To Burt -
Best wishes for all your
San Diego trails!
Linda Pyle

PACIFIC PEAKS & PICNICS

Day Journeys in San Diego County

by
Linda McMillin Pyle

Edited by
Evelyn Tschida McMillin

D1706522

Sunbelt Publications
San Diego, California

Pacific Peaks & Picnics: Day Journeys in San Diego County

Sunbelt Publications, Inc
Copyright © 2004 by Linda McMillin Pyle
All rights reserved. First edition 2004

Edited by Evelyn Tschida McMillin
Cover and Book Design by Leah Cooper
Project management by Jennifer Redmond
Printed in the United States of America

No part of this book may be reproduced in any form without permission from the publisher. Please direct comments and inquiries to:

Sunbelt Publications, Inc.
P.O. Box 191126
San Diego, CA 92159-1126
(619) 258-4911, fax: (619) 258-4916
www.sunbeltbooks.com

08 07 06 05 04   5 4 3 2 1

"Adventures in Natural History and Cultural Heritage"
A Series Edited by Lowell Lindsay

Library of Congress Cataloging-in-Publication Data

Pyle, Linda McMillin.
Pacific peaks & picnics : day journeys in San Diego County / by Linda McMillin Pyle ; edited by Evelyn Tschida McMillin.-- 1st ed.
    p. cm.
Includes bibliographical references and index.
ISBN 0-916251-66-7
1. San Diego County (Calif.)--Tours. 2. Scenic byways--California--San Diego County--Guidebooks. 3. Trails--California--San Diego County--Guidebooks. 4. Hiking--California--San Diego County--Guidebooks. 5. Natural history--California--San Diego County--Guidebooks. 6. Picnicking--California--San Diego County. 7. Cookery--California--San Diego County. I. Title: Pacific peaks and picnics. II. McMillin, Evelyn Tschida. III. Title.
F868.S15P95 2004
917.94'9804--dc22

                                        2004001925

Cover photo: Beach at Torrey Pines State Reserve in La Jolla
Cover Photo Credit: Celeste Daniels / Alamy
All other photos by Linda Pyle

Table of Contents

Acknowledgements

This book is a family affair beginning with a two week summer vacation road trip from Minnesota to California in 1957. Back then, up at 4 A.M each morning, we gulped down a Tang and toast breakfast and hit the road. Mom's itinerary included all the natural wonders, historic sites and city highlights. Dad put on 600 miles every day of travel on black-topped two-lane roads with my sister, brother and I in the backseat of a 1956 Ford. Lunch was a roadside picnic and a motel with a pool was a necessity for me.

Now as adults and California residents for over 20 years, we were back on the road again with my idea for this book. It could not have been written without Dad as our willing driver of endless miles and Mom becoming my invaluable editor and contributor.

My husband Scott (T.M. for Trail Master) has a unique gift; an uncanny and intuitive trail sense. His father, a forward artillery observer in the Korean War, taught him at the age of twelve how to navigate the Arizona desert by himself in a jeep. Without T.M.'s support and trail mastering, this book would not have been written.

Susan Senti contributed recipes and unending encouragement as did all the family and friends who helped us trail-test recipes.

Jennifer Redmond at Sunbelt Publications gave enthusiastic support and expert guidance. Her knowledge of regional publishing and publicity has been invaluable. I also wish to thank everyone at Sunbelt Publications for their expertise in distributing regional books.

Leah Cooper of Armadillo Creative created the beautiful cover, easy to read interior layout and map. I thank her for patience, flexibility, attention to detail and most of all for her wonderful talent for book design.

Many dedicated people of San Diego were instrumental in the conservation of the estuaries, coastal wetlands, historic sites, mountain forests, deserts and inland valleys we traveled. I thank them for their vision and dedication to preserving open space for future generations.

Steven L. Rucker, a Novato firefighter, lost his life in October of 2003 assisting southern California firefighters. I would like to dedicate this book to his memory and to all the other heroic people who valiantly fought the worst fire in San Diego history.

Linda Pyle

Introduction

Pacific Peaks & Picnics
is the travel narrative
of four travelers ages forty to seventy
out to explore the
desert, beaches, mountains and inland valleys
of San Diego highlighting the best places to
hike, bike, skate, walk and picnic

Each vignette gives travel routes for easy,
moderate or strenuous journeys
Included are recipes for simple campfire meals
and delicious trailside
sandwiches, salads and desserts

Infused with our culinary heritage, the
recipes are drawn from the daily fare of the coasts
of Spain, the Greek Isles and France
Trails and food shared with family and friends
give a deeper meaning to life

This unique book can lead you to
Discover Ballast Bay with Cabrillo
Trek an uncrowded Balboa Park Trail
Explore the most haunted house in America
Hike Presidio Park trails in Old Town

Meet an American Avocet
Cross the Tijuana River on a little-known beach trail
Witness one of the rarest pine trees on earth
Join the crowd on the Strand in Mission Beach
Walk a Crystal Pier in Pacific Beach

Stroll the white sand beaches of Coronado Island
Find the hideaway beaches and coves of La Jolla
Try tide chasing and stair stepping in Encinitas
Meditate at Swami's and
Surf San Onofre

Learn Kumeyaay Indian history along Mission Trails
Charge into the Mexican-American War
and San Diego pioneer history along the newest
trail of the San Dieguito River Park
Sweep down pastoral roads of San Pasqual Valley
Agricultural Preserve

Roll through the oak woodlands of Laguna Mountain
Experience the gold rush days in Julian
Tarry at the Mount Palomar Observatory and
walk bunchgrass meadow trails of Palomar Mountain

Discover extraordinary beauty
in Hellhole Canyon
and a rare elephant in the Anza-Borrego Desert

A short distance from crowded cities experience another world of
fossil-ridden cliffs, salt marshes, rivers,
native plants, birds, trees and mountain solitude
Come along---jump in anywhere

COME STEP INTO SAN DIEGO COUNTY

Bayside & Downtown San Diego Journeys

Beach & Coastal Journeys

Inland Valley & Mountain Journeys

Desert Journeys

Trail Locations

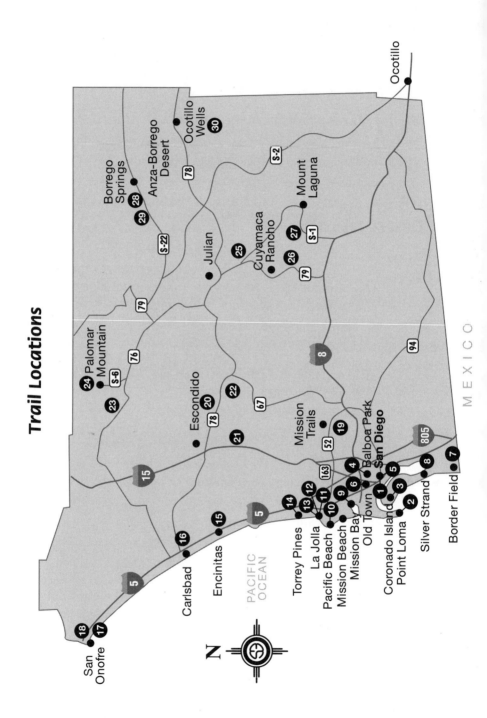

Map Key

Trail of San Diego Bay

*Skate San Diego Bay from Spanish Landing Park
to Embarcadero Marina Park*

丌

Cracked Peppercorn Chicken
Port Wine and Basil Butter on Crusty Bread

Our cruise ship the MS *Statendam* departs the Port of San Diego from the Broadway Pier. We stand on the highest deck of the ship and gaze back at the mountain peaks of the Peninsular Range that make a curvy organic frame for the city. Sunlight glints off the geometric shapes of the windows and roofs of the high-rise towers and skyscrapers.

Far below us in the ocean, the Coast Guard escorts us in a fast orange boat with a machine gun on the bow. The pilot gives us a friendly wave then zips ahead to cut off an approaching sailboat. The wide swath of our wake trails back toward the disappearing city.

A Canadian fellow traveler leans on the rail next to us and asks us to identify some of the harbor sights.

"That tip of land is Point Loma. It is the most southwestern point of the continental United States. See that place on the shoreline near the Submarine Base? It's called Ballast Bay. Cabrillo, the first European came ashore there in 1552."

Mom identifies the blue ribbon in the distance as the

San Diego Bay

1

engineering marvel, the Coronado Bridge. As we pass the last harbor buoy and enter the open Pacific Ocean I say, "This vision of downtown San Diego from the sea adds perspective to your impression of San Diego but to really know San Diego you have to get off the ship and experience it on foot."

My parents, my husband Scott (nicknamed T.M.) and I have been discovering San Diego on foot for the last thirteen years. And our first explorations started right here on the TRAIL OF SAN DIEGO BAY at Spanish Landing Park on the north side of the Bay next to Harbor Island.

On that day we are within earshot of the San Diego International Airport, yet the air is salty fresh. Networks of nearly five miles of connecting sidewalks lace the Bay and make for great walking or inline skating. Mom and Dad drop me at the curb. They prefer to sightsee by car and rendezvous later. I slip on kneepads, wrap wrist guards tight with a zip of the Velcro straps and snap on a helmet to begin a wobbly stride along Harbor Drive happy to be free of the car. Intermittent signs offer a self-guided tour around a portion of the Harbor.

Spanish Landing

At Spanish Landing Park I find a stretch of green grass on the water with an inviting picnic area and swimming beach. Today the placid ocean wraps San Diego like a soft baby-blue blanket. Tumultuous grand historical events happened here shaping the history of California and San Diego.

I screech my heel brake on the sidewalk and drag to a stop to read the Spanish Landing monument:

Spanish Landing Park

2

*"Near this point, sea and land parties of the
Portola-Serra expedition met. Two ships, the San
Antonio and San Carlos, anchored on May 4-5,
1769. The scurvy-weakened survivors of the
voyage established a camp where on May 14 and
July 1 they greeted the overland parties from Baja
California. Together they began the Spanish
occupation of Alta California."*

Father Junipero Serra

Two hundred and fifty years of human beaverlike activity
around the Bay have created smooth traveling for my journey.
Father Serra and company must have slogged through squishy,
soggy wetland swatting gnats and fleas as they toiled to get to
high ground about three miles from here. At the foot of Presidio
Hill, they established the first Franciscan Mission and Fort in
Alta, California. A Spanish style plaza surrounded by adobe
brick buildings provided a stopping point on the El Camino Real
along which Spain marched soldiers and missionaries north to
the Sonoma Mission by 1823. It was a short-lived occupation.

End of Spain's Pacific Reign

In the early 1820s Mexico successfully revolted against
Spain. They threw out the Crown and ended Spain's reign
over this Pacific coast forever. San Diego served as the
unofficial capital of Alta and Baja California for a few decades.

Then the Mexican people of the puebla welcomed ships
arriving from China, Boston, Hawaii, England and the
Philippines. They traded cowhides, called California bank
notes, for nails, dishes, tobacco, and oriental rugs. Fiestas and
weddings were celebrated on the plaza. But the winds of war
changed life for the Californios. By February of 1848, the
Americans had defeated the Mexicans. San Diego now
belonged to the Americans.

American Vision for the Bay

In front of me, the triangle of Point Loma looms large in the Bay. Pleasure boats and harbor excursions stream across the calm water. I had discovered how the Spanish and the Mexican people had contributed to San Diego. Now as the modern skyline of the city rises above me, I can see the American vision.

Alonzo Horton

One spring day in 1867, strong-willed Alonzo Horton disembarked from the paddle wheel steamer *Pacific* arriving from San Francisco. He saw San Diego as potentially the most important commercial shipping port and transportation hub in the Southwest! He banked on the importance of the port, shunned the Old Town and invested in almost one thousand acres of land that was three miles away on the Bay for less than three hundred dollars. Horton's "New Town," is now the center of modern bustling San Diego. Old Town is preserved as a State Historic Park.

The Embarcadero

As I pass the coast Guard Station, the blades of a helicopter whoosh as it lands. There is a crisp, shipshape naval presence to San Diego. It serves as homeport to some of the United States Pacific Fleet's surface ships, submarines, coastal patrol boats for SEALS and the aircraft carriers CONSTELLATION, JOHN C. STENNIS AND NIMITZ.

Maritime Museum

After about two and one-half miles I reach a stretch of waterfront that evokes memories of my first visit to San Diego in the 1960s. The tattoo parlors and sleazy sailor bars are gone but Anthony's Fish Grotto is still serving up delicious crab, shrimp and lobster next to the Maritime Museum.

Star of India

Star of India

Docked at the harbor museum the full-rigged *Star of India* marks a time when iron-hulled ships replaced the wooden ships that once ruled the seas and made voyages of discovery to this coast.

It is the oldest iron-hulled vessel still afloat and able to sail. Built in 1863, she was experimental as most ships were still being constructed of wood. This merchant ship symbolized a prosperous new life for the Irish, English and Scottish working class emigrants it transported from London to New Zealand. Although no one stands on deck today, the ship is not empty in my mind's eye. I see an Irishman waving goodbye to his family knowing he may never again return to the green hills of the Emerald Isle.

By 1923, steam ships dominated commerce and the sailing ship passed into oblivion. With the *Star of India* ready for the scrap yard, San Diego citizens preserved precious maritime history and established a landmark of San Diego.

The museum also exhibits the *Medea*, a still seaworthy steam yacht once owned by an eccentric millionaire and a turn-of-the-century ferryboat, the *Berkeley*, which was built in 1898. It transported passengers between Oakland and San Francisco for more than half a century.

Broadway Pier

Cruise ships now depart from the busy Broadway Pier. In 1935, Franklin D. Roosevelt embarked from this pier to deep-sea fish. As I wonder how many fish he caught, I trip when the red pavers catch my wheels.

Next I discover Tuna Harbor, a small peninsula with restaurants and a panoramic view and Seaport Village, 22 acres of shops, boutiques and restaurants.

Embarcadero Marina Park

On the final stretch of my harbor tour, at the Embarcadero Park I get a good view of the Coronado Bay Bridge. The Park attracts kids and parents pushing strollers. Business people power-walk past me on their way to work. I come to rest at the Hyatt and Marriott Hotels where the fins and sails of the Convention Center fill the sky. The Bay extends 17 miles all the way to Imperial Beach. But this is the end of the connecting sidewalks.

I rejoin Mom and Dad seated inside Anthony's Fish Grotto. From the window we watch cruise ships depart. We didn't know then that we would someday stand on the highest deck of the MS *Statendam* and tell a man from Canada about the sights of San Diego Bay.

~ Travel Notes ~

From Interstate 5 heading south, exit on Washington Street. Go onto Hancock St. Turn right onto W. Washington St. Turn left onto Pacific Highway. Turn right onto W. Hawthorn St. Turn right onto North Harbor Dr.

From Interstate 5 heading north, exit the Hawthorn exit toward San Diego airport. Keep left at the fork in ramp and merge onto W. Hawthorn St. Turn right onto North Harbor Dr.

Spanish Landing Park is on North Harbor Drive just west of San Diego Lindbergh Field airport. There are picnic tables available. From Spanish Landing follow along Harbor Drive east and then south to the Embarcadero, (end of Hawthorne Street), Maritime Museum, (end of Ash Street), the Broadway Pier, (end of Broadway), Seaport Village and Embarcadero Marina Park (end of Kettner Boulevard.)

For another great picnic spot, cross over to Coronado Island continue to follow Harbor Drive, take the Highway 75 exit to cross bridge. Coronado Tidelands Park is at the foot of 3rd Street along Mullinix Dr., north of the old tollbooth off Glorietta Boulevard. Picnic tables and benches are available on the lawn with sweeping views of the Bay.

Anthony's Fish Grotto is located at 1360 North Harbor Drive. "All San Diego Tours" harbor cruises depart from the Broadway Pier. Web site: www.allsandiegotours.com

Cracked Peppercorn Chicken

The chicken can be made the night before and served cold.

6 boneless, skinless chicken breasts
1 cup coarse Dijon mustard
4 cloves garlic, minced
2 teaspoons cracked peppercorns
2 teaspoons dried sage
½ cup grated Parmesan cheese

Preheat oven to 350°. Place chicken breasts in baking dish in single layer.

Mix together mustard, garlic and peppercorns. Spoon mixture onto chicken breasts. Sprinkle with dried sage and Parmesan cheese.

Bake about 45 minutes or until juices run clear when pricked with a fork. Refrigerate.

Pack in cooler or insulated bag for beach. Serve chicken over a bed of greens topped with vinaigrette made with equal parts of olive oil and lemon juice with sprinkle of sugar.

Serves 4-6.

Port Wine and Basil Butter

2 teaspoons Port wine
¼ pound butter
1 teaspoon basil, finely chopped

Soften butter to room temperature. Stir in wine and basil. Refrigerate.

Serve on crusty bread.

Trail of Cabrillo

Visit Cabrillo National Monument, walk the Bayside Trail
Ballast Bay, Point Loma

茶

Portuguese Fish Stew
Mediterranean Bread

We stand 400 feet above the San Diego coastal plain on the most extreme southwestern tip of land in the continental United States. The turbulent Pacific Ocean batters the yellow cliffs below us on the west flank. The calmer San Diego Bay laps Point Loma on the east flank.

This green point of land covered with chaparral remained outside the known mapped world until September of 1552, when the first European expedition to the coast of North America stepped onto its shore.

Juan Rodriquez Cabrillo

Jubilation and foreboding must have filled the soul of Juan Rodriguez Cabrillo as he surveyed this headland from his flagship galleon, the *San Salvador*. Curiosity and dread must have filled the hearts of the Kumeyaay Indians as they blinked in disbelief at the "houses on the sea," two caravels and a galleon, flying the blood-red cross of Spain. The Pueblo Indians and Yuman people to the east had already told them terrifying stories of bearded soldiers wielding spears and cross bows. They now witnessed these strange mythical conquistadors invading their peaceful bay.

The bountiful shores of the Bay were one of eight permanently established homes to itinerant Indian tribes. At the time of Juan Rodriquez Cabrillo's landing, San Diego's native population was estimated to be about 20,000 strong: Luiseno, Cahuilla, Cupeno, Kumeyaay and Northern Diegueno. Shellfish, nuts and berries provided a bountiful life.

For many explorers what they seek is not necessarily what they find. Ordered north up the coast of New Spain (Mexico) by the King of Spain and the Viceroy of New Spain, Cabrillo was to search for a legendary river connecting the Pacific and Atlantic Oceans. At that time modern wisdom held that California was an island perhaps inhabited by Amazon women. He was to lay claim to all of the land. As he pushed north into Alta California, he went farther than any Spanish explorer had ever gone.

Favorable Winds

His courage had been tested as a younger man. He helped to conquer Guatemala and wielded a crossbow against the Aztecs. Cabrillo, already well-to-do, left behind his previous life as miner, merchant and landowner to command a fleet of ships he himself had built for coastal exploration. Three months out of Navidad, Mexico, traveling many leagues and enduring "impeding cross winds, terrible weather, dangerous shallows and reefs, showers, sudden shifts in wind and let ups," favorable winds finally propelled him into the great curve of today's San Diego Bay. Staying only six days while waiting out a storm before sailing farther up the coast, Cabrillo christened the gentle bay, San Miguel.

Cabrillo National Monument

On the TRAIL OF CABRILLO, we seek the glory and passion of the great explorer with a climb by car up the hilly streets of ship-shape Point Loma, reaching the plateau of this high, jagged peninsula now occupied by Fort Rosecrans National Cemetery.

We pass identical white head stones that cross rolling green hills in symmetrical rows. After the Mexican-American

War, the U.S. Army First Dragoons killed in the battle of San Pasqual were reburied here. Over 49,000 American military service people and their families are also honored here. My husband's parents are both buried near the obelisk.

Panoramic Overlook

Visitor Center

The sun struggles to penetrate a sky roofed with gray clouds outside the Cabrillo Visitor Center. A foghorn blasts dull and lonely, adding to the morning gloom.

Inside, exhibits show Cabrillo's voyage in large dioramas. A model of his ship *San Salvador* reveals that although only about 100 feet long and 25 feet wide, a crew of around one hundred slaves, sailors and soldiers ate, slept, worked and perhaps prayed on deck next to sheep, horses and chickens. Good teeth were a necessity for sailors to gnaw on hardtack biscuits and salted dried meats. Only Cabrillo and perhaps, Bartolme Ferrelo, chief pilot of the *Victoria*, might have had the luxury of private quarters.

Unsolved Mystery

As he was known to have been a literate man, I picture Cabrillo writing in the ship's navigational journal by candlelight. His logs have never been found. Accounts of the expedition have been pieced together by surviving crewmembers and historian conjecture. Cabrillo's life is an unsolved mystery. No one knows his exact age, whether his face was handsome or brutish, or even if he was Spanish or Portuguese!

Sweeping Views

Beyond the glass walls of the Visitor Center, a sweeping view of San Diego floats dizzily. After thumbing and purchasing books, we sign the logbook along with travelers from Japan, Spain, Germany and the United Kingdom.

Like a kid on a school field trip, I am anxious to run the Bayside Trail down to Ballast Bay, the very spot where Cabrillo first made claim to this coastline for Spain. But first we explore the old lighthouse nearby with an easy walk up a road.

The Old Lighthouse

The old lighthouse

Until 1855, this headland held no warning foghorn, welcoming beacon or cozy New England style lighthouse. The original lighthouse, in which we now stand, answered the demand for safer passage along the then well-traveled coast. Captain Israel, once a keeper of the light, trimmed the wicks, cleaned the glass and polished the brass. His family's few comforts on display speak of hardship. A bumpy, nine-mile wagon ride into town for supplies isolated the family.

Shipwrecks

On a clear night sailors took heed of the beacon reaching 39 miles. But today, low hanging clouds remind of the fog which often plagued Captain Israel's lighthouse and caused unfortunate shipwrecks. A new one, constructed closer to the water in 1891, is now fully automated and still operational.

Bayside Trail to Ballast Bay

At last my chance comes to breeze down the old Army road for the two-mile round trip trail to Ballast Bay. The moderate decline drops 300 hundred feet. I pass Mom and Dad as they stop to explore the military bunkers built as part of a protective ring of defense for the Harbor during World Wars I and II.

Native Coastal Sage Scrub

The native Coastal Sage Scrub I pass attracts me with its haunting beauty. The Lemonadeberry and Coastal Sagebrush are the unique essence of southern California. There is great pleasure in witnessing the California Encelia that shines like a thousand yellow suns. Or the Prickly-pear cactus protected by fierce spines. These valuable endemic plants are preserved and protected in the Point Loma Ecological Reserve. Graceful deer and swift little cottontail rabbits hidden by this dense underbrush would have made mouthwatering delicacies for Cabrillo's crew.

Acts of Possession

At last, the low clouds depart. Down at Ballast Bay, I stand in sunlight. Picking up a smooth stone, I think of Cabrillo declaring this land for Spain. Perhaps he moved stones from one pile to another or gathered water from the Bay in a clay vessel and poured it out on the land. These were customary acts of possession in his day, like our astronauts planting the American flag on the moon.

Spirit of Place

The spirit of place illuminates history like the flickering candle did in Cabrillo's private quarters on the *San Salvador*. I understand the passion and glory of an explorer and the confusion and fear of the native people of Alta California as I stand on this spot. Cabrillo's exhilaration and Kumeyaay dread are still electric presences in the rolling momentum of the unstoppable ocean waves piercing the terrible beauty of the sandstone cliffs. I turn to look back out to sea and imagine the three ships disappearing on the far horizon.

Cabrillo's Last Days

Cabrillo in his day must have had the status of today's astronaut. But his rising star faded quickly. Shipmate's journals reflect that before a year had passed, his lifeless body, ravaged by gangrene, would lie buried on a windswept Channel Island. Again a mystery, scholars don't agree whether a broken arm or leg killed him or even on which Channel Island he is buried. It is known that Bartolme Ferrelo, chief pilot of the *Victoria*, was ordered to carry on the exploration.

Captain Sebastian Vizcaino

Sixty years later, Captain Sebastian Vizcaino, attempted to claim discovery of Cabrillo's former findings along the coast by renaming Cabrillo's discovery San Miguel, San Diego, usurping for a time, Cabrillo's rightful place in history. But Cabrillo, the conquistador, has not been forgotten. His greatest accomplishments are immortalized here at Cabrillo National Monument.

~ Travel Notes ~

Cabrillo National Monument is located at the tip of Point Loma at the end of State Highway 209 (also called Catalina Boulevard.) From Interstate 5 south or I-8 west exit at Rosecrans/209 exit. Follow Rosecrans, make a right on Canon St. and left on Catalina Blvd. From Interstate 5 north, exit and go left on Hawthorne St. then right on N. Harbor Drive, left on Rosecrans St., right on Canon St. and left on Catalina Blvd.

Admission fee: $5.00 per car, $2.00 per person for cyclists and walk-ins. Open daily at 9 a.m. Web Site: www.nps.gov/cabr/home.html

Bayside Trail is 2 miles round trip. There are benches at Cabrillo National Park but no cooking facilities or picnic tables.

Portuguese Fish Soup

The Portuguese were the first to write recipes into cookbooks. Using clam juice instead of fish stock makes this recipe fast to prepare. The sailors probably used dried cod.

2 pounds of fish such as cod,
halibut, haddock, shrimp, sea scallops
1 cup chopped onion
3 cloves minced garlic
1 tablespoon olive oil
16 ounces clam juice
1 cup of a dry white wine
1 pound chopped Roma tomatoes
⅛ teaspoon each dried thyme and basil
¼ bay leaf
Freshly ground black pepper to taste

In a large kettle sauté onion and garlic in olive oil for 5 minutes. Add clam juice and wine and bring to a boil.

Reduce heat and add fish to pot. Add tomatoes, thyme, basil, bay leaf and pepper. Gently simmer 5 minutes or more until fish is cooked.

Pack for the park in wide mouth thermos. Bring spoons and bowls.

Garnish with chopped parsley. Serve with Mediterranean bread.

Serves 4.

Mediterranean Bread

1 tablespoon fast rising yeast
1 tablespoon sugar
1½ cup lukewarm water
1 cup lukewarm milk
1½ cup cornmeal
5½ cups flour
2½ tablespoons olive oil
1½ tablespoon salt

Dissolve yeast and sugar in warm water in a small bowl.

In a large warmed non-metal bowl stir together 1 cup flour, 1 cup cornmeal and yeast mixture. Beat until smooth. Cover with a light cloth and let rest 45 minutes in a slightly warmed spot.

Stir in milk, oil and salt. Fold in all cornmeal and enough remaining flour to form a ball. Knead on a floured board 5 minutes. Place back in bowl and allow to rest covered 45 minutes.

Punch down and shape into 2 balls. Place into 2 lightly oiled cake pans pressing dough to spread to edges. Allow to rise 45 minutes.

In a 450° preheated oven bake for 15 minutes spraying 3 or 4 times during baking with water to create a crispy top. Bake 15 minutes more reducing heat to 400°.

Serve with butter or jam.

Trail of the Victorian Lady

*Visit to the Hotel Del Coronado and skate
Coronado City Beach, Coronado Island*

⊼

S'mores
Toasted Campfire Snowballs
Bonfire Candied Apples
Hot Mexican Chocolate

Southern California has its own turn-of-the-century castle!
And this Victorian hotel built with wood, designed with
bright red turrets and cupolas, commands the white Coronado
beaches like a grand
ageless lady. The
Hotel Del Coronado,
built in 1888 by
Hampton Story
and Elisha Spurr
Babcock, Jr.,
still emanates an
irresistible charm.
Why has this "lady"
remained steadfast
and popular,

Hotel Del Coronado

surviving the wrecking ball and the desire to replace the old
with the new? The answer comes from the past from two
visionary men whose daydreams led them to an extraordinary
undertaking.

Hotel Del Coronado

On the TRAIL OF THE VICTORIAN LADY, the story
of these men unfolds as we enter the lobby of the hotel. Two

friends, Hampton Story from a piano tycoon family and Elisha Babcock recently retired from the railroad, hailed from the Midwest.

Babcock's doctor had given him the prescription of the day for tuberculosis: "Go west and rest in a good climate." At the age of 34 he moved to San Diego. Often he and Story would row out to the San Diego peninsula to fish for sea perch and hunt jackrabbits along a pristine white sand spit.

Historic Conversation

After one particularly memorable day of leisure, a historic conversation between them began. "We ought to build a hotel, Story, the brightest, smartest hostelry on any coast. We ought to build it on that spot across the bay where we sunburned this morning." Thus the dream began.

Babcock speculated that soon the trains would bring many Easterners to enjoy the moderate San Diego climate and that they would be willing to pay for luxury and comfort.

A Bold Plan

Hatching a bold plan, the pair purchased what would become the Coronado and North Island property for $110,000. Babcock described their vision vividly to the architects to be "the talk of the western world!" The perfect location chosen, the challenges began.

Building the dream

There were no utilities, infrastructure or transportation on Coronado. Coastal Sage Scrub was cleared and water piped in from the San Diego River. They enlisted Thomas Edison to travel from the East to guide them in building a generator. Electricity was still a novel luxury and not deemed to last! Streets were laid out and ferry wharves built. Wanting the very latest luxuries for their guests, the men personally made sure the new-fangled telephone would ring at the hotel.

Hunting Lodge by the Sea

I climb the stairs and surreptitiously watch guests registering in the lobby below just like the ladies of the last century. When the first guests came to the "hunting lodge by the sea," they found no carpet and spittoons adorned the lobby of the hotel. Then, the gallery on which I stand allowed women to observe the comings and goings of the hunters and fisherman without being seen. The Del even had a woman's entrance designed so the ladies, windblown from the beach or dusty from excursions, could slip unnoticed into their rooms for repair.

History Gallery

Downstairs in the History Gallery, we learn that over the last one hundred years, this wonder of a hotel has attracted 14 Presidents including Roosevelt, Kennedy, Bush and Clinton as well as the last Hawaiian monarch, King Kalakaua.

Marilyn Monroe, Tony Curtis and Jack Lemon were here to film *Some Like It Hot* under the direction of Billy Wilder. Authors Henry James and L. Frank Baum, of Wizard of Oz fame, were inspired to write here. New York publisher John Pulitzer was one of the first guests. Royalty was hosted when Edward, Prince of Wales visited. And the Duke of Windsor reputedly first met Wallace Simpson here, the Coronado housewife for whom he gave up the throne of England.

Coronado Shores Beach

Outside on the white sandy beach we walk down the coast to Coronado Shores. The thatched cabana huts of the famous Tent City are now gone. Tent City sprang up along the Silver Strand, south of the hotel while renovations were being made to the Del in 1902. Then, music from the plays, concerts and vaudeville shows filled the air. Indoor saltwater plunges were all the rage where the less well-heeled cooled off next to the opulent hotel.

Coronado City Beach

A naval plane lands in North Island with a roar. I skate along the Coronado City Beach with a thought of Charles Lindbergh taking off in the Spirit of St. Louis in 1927 from this Naval Air Station. Amelia Earhart flew from here and others made first seaplane flights and a first parachute jump.

Along the sidewalk where I skate, boulders are piled high. This sea wall was constructed back in 1906. Beach goers loll on the white sand and comb for shells—a perfect place for a picnic.

The long tradition of picnics on Coronado started with Isabel Babcock and Della Story celebrating under the new pavilion on July 4, 1886.

Skates off, I walk down to the white sand spit. The harsh afternoon sun glares on the ocean.

Talk of the Western World

This turn-of the-century hotel is a window into another century, a taste of a bygone era of leisure time and travel. Boldly undertaken by two men of vision, its lasting beauty is truly ageless.

~ Travel Notes ~

From downtown San Diego exit Interstate 5 at Highway 75 and cross the Coronado Bridge. Pass the toll plaza and turn left at Orange Ave. Proceed to the Hotel del Coronado at 1500 Orange Ave. From Imperial Beach, take Highway 75 to Orange Ave. Coronado City Beach is west of Ocean Boulevard. The fire rings are located at the north end of the beach.

S'mores

1 box of plain graham crackers
1 package of Hershey chocolate bars
1 bag of regular size marshmallows

Bring sticks or long skewers for roasting marshmallows. After the fire has developed some glowing coals, toast until golden or set on fire and blacken to your taste. Slip the marshmallows between the graham crackers and chocolate bar. Pull out the stick and squish together.

For a sinfully rich variation use brownies cut in half horizontally instead of graham crackers. Reese's candy can be substituted for a peanut butter taste or peppermint patties for a mint flavor. Sliced strawberries add freshness.

Toasted Campfire Snowballs

1 8-inch angel food cake cut in 2-inch cubes
1 can sweetened condensed milk
½ cup coconut

Just before toasting, roll the cake in sweetened condensed milk and then in coconut. Thread on skewers and toast quickly, turning frequently over the fire until light brown.

Makes approximately 20.

Bonfire Candied Apples

8 apples, Macintosh, Jonathan or Granny Smith
1 cup brown sugar

Skewer apples at the stem end. Roast over coals until skin blackens and peels off easily. Roll hot apple in brown sugar, coating well. Return to the fire, turn slowly until sugar caramelizes.

Hot Mexican Chocolate

This chocolate can be found in the Mexican food section of the market.

6 cups milk
2 tablets sweet Mexican chocolate

Heat milk until very hot but not boiling. Pour hot milk into blender and add chocolate tablets. Blend together.

Heat thermos by rinsing with hot water and immediately pour chocolate into thermos. Serve in mugs.

Makes 4 servings.

Trail of Balboa Park

*Walk through California Native Plant Garden, Hike Florida
Canyon Trail, Visit to San Diego Historical Society and Walks
through Palm Canyon, Old Desert Garden, Japanese Friendship
Garden, Rose Garden and Desert Garden*

Ħ

Greek Salad in a Pita

Rain-soaked and hungry, we peek into the warm elegant
dining room. Could we go in wet and bedraggled? T.M.
peels off backpack and rain jacket. I stomp mud from my
hiking boots. Greeted as if dressed in our Sunday best, we are
whisked to a good table by the hostess. Smoothing damp hair,
T.M. smiles, "Did you ever think we'd be hiking off the Florida
Canyon Trail and into a gourmet restaurant today?"

Florida Canyon, Native Plant Garden

On the TRAIL OF BALBOA PARK we had driven south
with a slow-moving Pacific storm from Alaska on our tail.
Now, fat drops splatter on the windshield as we park on the
east side of Balboa Park near Dog Park.

Determined to hike the Florida Canyon Trail, we pull on
rain jackets and hurry around the California Native Plant
Garden. It promotes the use of native plants and trees of the
habitats of southern California: Chaparral, Woodland and
Riparian Coastal Sage Scrub. A benefit of planting these
aromatic drought-resistant plants is that they attract
pollinating bees, birds and butterflies. I recognize the purple-
flowered Cleveland Sage and Our Lord's Candle, a spiny
succulent like the one we have planted in our backyard.

25

Florida Canyon Trail

To get to the Florida Canyon Trail we hurry through Dog Park. Once on the Trail, the welcome rain intensifies the scent of the dark green-leafed Black Sage and fine gray-leafed Coastal Sagebrush. The Trail meanders along the hillsides east of the improved section of Balboa Park just miles from downtown San Diego. The still-natural urban hillsides have me remembering being a kid and sliding down golden hills on pieces of cardboard in the summer. We walk south along the natural dry landscape paralleling Florida Drive. This Trail preserves a glimpse of the look of the original land on which Balboa Park was developed.

Desert Garden

We cross Florida Drive at Zoo Place and traverse a dry wash that I surmise rarely gets water. We slog up to the Desert Garden where the Trail ends and manicured, sidewalked Balboa Park begins. I compose a picture of T.M. next to an old tangle of Euphorbia limbs hanging over his head like tentacles. Though it wasn't in today's plan we are so close to the heart of Balboa Park on the Plaza de Panama, lunch is on our minds.

It is our good fortune to stumble upon The Prado restaurant just as the rain gushes in a downpour sending everyone for shelter.

After lunch on the return trip back down the Florida Canyon Trail at the intersection of Zoo Place and Florida Drive, we head north taking a loop route to the car to avoid the dry wash, now a surging river of water.

Barrel Cactus, Desert Garden

Tree Gazing on a Return Trip

A few weeks later I bring Mom and Dad to explore more of the Park. We have arrived without a plan. We snap pictures of one ornate Spanish Colonial building, the Casa Del Prado Theater. Should we visit the Aerospace Museum, the Natural History Museum? With over a dozen museums, all inside a Park bigger than Central Park in New York, we can't decide. That is when our tree gazing begins.

The grand Moreton Bay Fig tree, planted in 1915, grows between the Natural History Museum and Spanish Village. It welcomes visitors today with a sheltering canopy 120 feet wide and 60 feet high!

Many of the oldest and tallest trees populating the Park are eucalyptus of the myrtle family. Limpid scythe-like evergreen leaves are aromatic and used for oils and medicinal purposes.

The west side of the Park contrasts with the Florida Canyon native dry landscape thanks to Kate Sessions, the pioneer horticulturist dubbed the "Mother of Balboa Park."

In 1892 she started planting exotic and non-native trees. Many pepper, acacia, cypress and eucalyptus were planted, with respect for the natural site and dry climate.

Finding ourselves at the Casa de Balboa building, we tour the free San Diego Historical Society, a mosaic of San Diego history and traveling exhibitions. After a brief stop at the Visitor Center for a map, hunger has us waiting for The Prado on the Plaza de Panama to open. Plein air artists paint the carved limestone fountain called *Woman of Tehuantepec* in the courtyard filled with orange clivia and palms as we wait.

Prado opens. Mom points to the unusual chandeliers fashioned from deer antlers and filled with red, blue, orange and yellow art glass shapes.

"That's how I feel about the Park—I see a kaleidoscope of natural and manmade jewels."

After lunch, out in the courtyard the painting teacher lines the canvases up for critique. Joining a small crowd of amateur critics, we judge. All masterpieces, we agree.

Palm Canyon

Palm Canyon is my pick for our next tree gazing foray. The sun breaks through. The sky above the statue of El Cid is a soldier blue. "Drove the Moors out of Spain." Mom recalls.

An unseen clock chimes the hour of one as we enter nearby Palm Canyon via a wooden footbridge. As we galumph along I turn on the tape recorder to record the constant and ever present peep, cheep and warbling of Park birds.

Holding the recorder, I say "Maybe this will pick up our footsteps too."

"Pick up the pace? Speed up! You need to slow down and—."

"No, I said talking louder, "Pick up the sound of our footsteps on the bridge."

We descend laughing into the shady cool canyon of the palms. I do walk fast. They prefer a slow meandering.

"Look at the ghostly fingers of the Moreton Bay fig. The roots look like feet to me."

Sun glints on bright green silly topknots of palm fronds atop the slender trunks of Mexican Fanpalms. These trees are over one hundred years old.

We come to a split in the trail of the tropical forest. Dad quotes Yogi Berra, "When you come to a fork in the road take it!"

Moreton Bay Fig tree roots, Palm Canyon Trail

Old Cactus Garden

So up the muddy left fork we go and wind up at the back of the Balboa Park Club. Picnic tables are set in the Old Cactus Garden. We examine some specimens of succulents and cacti that are the oldest and largest in the Park planted in the early 1900s Kate Sessions planned this garden for the 1935 Exposition.

Japanese Friendship Garden

As we head back toward the Rose Garden on the east side, the clock chimes 2:00. Impulsively we are drawn into the tranquil Japanese Friendship Garden. Pink and white azaleas bloom profusely. In a *Shi-Shi-Odoshi* a bamboo pole hits a stone with a clack and drops water, keeping evil spirits away. Mom remarks she admires the controlled and simple Japanese landscaping as well as the ornate Spanish architecture and gardens.

Our voices echo inside the wood and glass Tea Pavilion. I melt into a garden bench to drink in the peace. Mom lags behind taking pictures of a stone lantern and bonsai trees. This garden achieves a "nearly perfect blend of nature, peace and tranquility," as promised.

We linger, sipping tea and tasting almond cookies. Mom and Dad reminisce about trips to Japan. The clock chimes three times.

We stroll back to El Prado, turn right and head toward the Bea Evenson fountain. We cross over Park Boulevard on a white pedestrian bridge and step into a bed of roses—three acres of roses in full bloom.

Reaching the Desert Garden, located next to the Rose Garden, we come full circle to the garden T.M. and I had explored that day in the rain.

On the way home, I think of that antler chandelier in The Prado. This Park truly is an eclectic joining of natural and man-made objects. On both trips we chose to explore the natural aspect of the Park. We spent hours walking through dry knee-high sages, under towering palm trees, around beds of roses and skirting prickly cactus and spiky succulents. The unexplored manmade objects call us back again to Balboa Park.

~ Travel Notes ~

From southbound Interstate 5 exit at 10th Ave., turn left on "A" St. and left again on Park Blvd. Look for Balboa Park signs.

From northbound Interstate 5 exit B Street/Pershing Drive. Take Pershing Dr. and go left at Florida Drive. Turn left at Zoo Place to Park Blvd. Take a left on Park Blvd.

To start at Florida Canyon were this hike begins from either Park Blvd. or Florida Dr. turn right on Morley Field Dr. Turn right at the top of the hill near tennis courts, Native Plant Demonstration Garden and dog park.

The Florida Canyon Trail starts south of the native plant garden and tennis courts. To follow our route head south paralleling Florida Dr. Cross over Florida Dr. where Zoo Place intersects. Follow the Trail up through Desert Garden. To return go back to the intersection of Zoo Place and Florida Dr. and go left or north paralleling Florida Dr. back to the parking area near tennis courts.

The San Diego Historical Society is at the Casa De Balboa building. Admission fee: donation. The Visitor Center is in the House of Hospitality on the Plaza de Panama at the heart of the Park. Open 9:00 a.m.-4:00 p.m. Exhibit admission fees vary. Information: www.balboapark.org

To follow our tree gazing tour: the Moreton Bay fig tree is between the Spanish Village and the Natural History Museum. Proceed to the Plaza de Panama. Walk south to the entrance to Palm Canyon and follow the trail to the Old Cactus Garden behind the Balboa Park Club. Pass the International Cottages, the United Nations and Hall of Nations buildings to the Japanese Friendship Garden near the Organ Pavilion, admission $3. From there, proceed back to the Plaza De Panama and head east to the Bea Evenson Fountain and cross the footbridge over Park Blvd. The Rose Garden is to the south and the Desert Garden to the north.

Scenic picnic spots are everywhere throughout the Park. The Prado at Balboa Park restaurant is in the House of Hospitality across the courtyard from the Visitor Center.

Greek Salad in a Pita

1½ heads romaine lettuce
1 peeled cucumber, sliced thinly
½ sliced red onion
4 tomatoes, diced and drained
12 ounces feta cheese, crumbled
20 Kalamata olives, drained

Dressing:
½ cup fresh lemon juice
½ cup olive oil
½ teaspoon marjoram
½ teaspoon oregano
3 cloves garlic, minced
Salt and freshly ground pepper to taste

Pita bread, halved

Wash, dry and tear romaine into small pieces. Prepare all vegetables and place in container. Pack another container with tomatoes, feta cheese and olives.

To make dressing, mix together in a shakeable container, lemon juice, olive oil, oregano, marjoram, garlic, salt and fresh ground pepper to taste.

Just before serving, place the romaine and remaining ingredients into a large wooden bowl. Shake the dressing well and toss salad. Offer fresh ground pepper to taste. Serve in pita bread.

Serves 4-6 as a main course.

Trail of Haunted San Diego

Ghosts and Grave Stones Trolley Tour: William Heath Davis Home and Villa Montezuma in downtown San Diego and Campo Santo Cemetery and Whaley House in Old Town

Ħ

Victorian Ginger Nuts

O n a Saturday night we assemble outside the William Heath Davis house in the Gaslamp District, downtown San Diego. Our Ghosts and Gravestones tour guide gathers us into a circle on the TRAIL OF HAUNTED SAN DIEGO. He reveals, "If it were the 1880s and we ventured into the "stingaree" of San Diego near the waterfront where we are now, being knifed, shot or clubbed and waking up on a ship sailing for Singapore or Shanghai would have been a definite risk!"

Ghosts and Gravestones Tour

Our old-time undertaker for the evening, dressed in rumpled black suit with vest over white shirt, string tie askew and black slouch hat, soon gets to what is on everyone's mind, even the kid wearing a plastic miners hat: will we see a ghost tonight?

"Don't know tonight how we will experience the spirit world."

But he confides that just last week a visitor photographed orbs, just two weeks ago someone captured plasma fogs on film and just two Sundays ago several women on this tour were invited by a mysterious tour guide dressed in white to see the third floor of the Davis house we are about to enter. Nothing unusual about that except the upper floor is off limits and no tour guide of this world works up there. "Feel for cold spots," he says.

William Heath Davis House

My tape recorder rolling and camera in hand, we crowd down into the hot, dark basement of the William Heath Davis home with twenty other ghost busters.

Standing in dim light he divulges that this house is "the oldest surviving structure from San Diego's New Town." Shipped from the East Coast around Cape Horn and assembled in San Diego in 1850, this prefabricated "salt-box" was home to soldiers, a German spy and Alonzo Horton and his wife Sarah. But Davis never lived here; his home was also a salt-box identical to this family home. After a decline in the San Diego economy, most remaining prefabs were burned for firewood or moved.

Activating the green light inside Casper, the ghost pins we wear to prevent us from being shanghaied by a specter, we file upstairs past a parlor filled with Victorian furniture and period clothing. No otherworldly tour guide invites us to the third floor so we tramp outside. Solemnly we are ushered onto a trolley draped in black crepe. A noose hangs for the driver to ring a clanging bell.

Ghost of Horton Grand Hotel

From the trolley windows, we crane our necks to stare up to the third floor of the Horton Grand Hotel. Our guide has first-hand knowledge that room 309 is possessed with the spirit of a gambler named Roger. Reportedly Roger was shot in the Bucket of Blood or the Acme Bar after reneging on gambling debts. Managing to crawl back to room 309, his assailants followed the bloody trail and discovered him hiding in a closet and finished him off. Our host reports when he himself stayed in the room, he personally woke up to mysterious occurrences: decks of cards laid out by their suits, coins stacked like poker chips and the closet door opening by itself. Now we have no doubts as to our guide's credentials as a ghost hunter!

The trolley climbs above downtown San Diego while we garner some history about efforts of San Diegans to improve the city's reputation and rid the "scrappage" of things, murderers and roughnecks,

Two brother promoters hatched a plan: entice the most famous piano player in the world, Jesse Shepard, to come live in San Diego and promise him a dream house he could keep. It worked.

Villa Montezuma

At K and 20th up on a hill, the lights of San Diego shimmer on the horizon as we enter Villa Montezuma named after the ship that brought Jesse from England to America— a custom of the day.

Inside the Queen Anne-style Victorian painted pink and green, Jesse stares back at us from a photograph. The mahogany paneled room is hot.

The last light of sundown filters through windows of exquisite painted art glass illuminating the faces of playwrights Shakespeare and Corneille and composers Mozart and Beethoven.

Lights down low, creepy organ music playing, we move into the piano salon where spiritualist Jesse, piano player to the royalty of Europe, would claim to channel the music of the long-dead composers during his séances in this very parlor. It was the hottest show in the boom town days of New Town.

The house may have bestowed some temporary glamour to San Diego but never brought prosperity to those connected to it. "All associated with it died in abject poverty," our guide says sadly. Jesse left San Diego after a very short time. His extravagant tastes in home building eventually left the promoters penniless.

Back on the bus we remark that the priceless art glass windows, visible from the street, have never been vandalized. Some say protected by a black-clad apparition who watches the neighborhood from the turret.

We rattle in our hearse-designed bus on the freeway away from New Town to the heart of Old Town and debark at the

El Campo Santo pioneer cemetery. Mexican music spills out of the many restaurants along San Diego Avenue.

El Campo Santo Cemetery

Our intrepid guide, lantern in hand, fascinates us with stories of the last century's burial customs. Evidently, burial near the center of the cemetery had the most status. The white pickets on paling fences around graves kept predators away from shallow burials but later the height of the paling itself came to symbolize the status of the dead and he points to some that rose to impractical heights.

In the late 1800s doctors couldn't always tell if a person was dead or comatose. Bells were rigged up over the grave so if someone were buried alive they could ring and be helped out by someone hired to sit in the cemetery at night "working the graveyard shift." We recall Poe's *House of Usher*, maybe more reality than a horror story, we realize.

Our feet scrape slowly along the cemetery dirt. It is too dark to read the head stones. We congregate around the grave of Yankee Jim Robinson, infamous for stealing a man's horse then daring the owner to prove it to be his own. This arrogant horse thief raised the stakes and plotted to steal a schooner, got caught, was convicted and hung in the gallows yard. The rope too long, his death was a horrible thing for San Diegans to witness. The gallows grounds were just up the street, the lot on which the Whaley House is built.

Villa Montezuma

The Whaley House

Standing under a pepper tree an involuntary shiver runs between my shoulder blades. Someone pounds a board with a hammer. Constructing the gallows? I am the first of our group to walk into the most haunted house in the United States, tape recorder on and camera in hand. Nervous laughter fills the parlor of the oldest brick home in San Diego. I don't smell Mr. Whaley's cigar smoke or Mrs. Whaley's melancholy lavender perfume. The musty smell of mold tells the story of a long-closed-up building.

Thomas Whaley

Thomas Whaley (1823-1890) sailed to California from New York for the gold rush and ended up opening the first brickyard in San Diego. But tragedy befell the Whaley family, the deaths of three of their children by suffocation, suicide and illness. Other strange deaths of people associated with the house also occurred in this residence built over the city gallows. Some people standing under the doorway between the sitting room and the music room have felt breathing restriction. Could it be because the house was built on the very spot where Yankee Jim Robinson hung from the gallows?

The house served as a residence, general store and still is furnished as a courtroom. Our feet clatter along the wood floor and chairs creak as we are ushered into the courtroom to view pictures of orbs, spheres, wisps of ectoplasm and full body materializations caught by digital cameras in the house.

"Mr. Whaley, a residual haunt," the curator says "stands in the dining room threshold to see who has come into his house." Those with digital cameras are urged to capture his image. Without 400 or 800 speed film it is doubtful I will capture anything from this "pinnacle of haunts." The Whaley House and the Winchester Mystery House in San Jose, have the distinction of being the only officially designated haunted houses as deemed by the U.S. Commerce Department.

Too soon, the driver pulls the noose and the trolley bell calls us back to the bus where several people polled say they have captured images in the house.

Pleased with the tour, our imagination piqued, we arrive back in the Gaslamp district. The "stingaree" streets are packed with ordinary patrons. Inside the Horton Grand Hotel, I run into the girl on our tour with a digital camera in hand playing back her images of Mr. Whaley. I drag T.M. over to see the negative image of a man in a black frock coat and vest wearing a wide-brimmed hat. We can't believe the image is so strikingly clear.

Skeptics, Mom and Dad wait for us in the car. "Pure hogwash, trickery" they say, "rigged up to hornswaggle you."

At home I play back my tape. Nothing unusual except in the Whaley house what sounds like the crackle and snap of a wood fire. Nothing, not an orb or plasma flow, in the photos.

Mom phones the next day to say maybe a ghost followed her home last night to dispute her disbelief. Seems she woke up in the middle of the night and went down to the kitchen, only to be startled by the green ghost still glowing on the lapel of her jacket!

Do ghosts haunt San Diego? Two thumbs up. Two thumbs down. Mom and Dad report that they suspended their skepticism of paranormal claims to enjoy the architecture of the homes visited and were amused by the stories told. We agree the Ghosts and Gravestones Tour makes learning a little history of Old and New Town San Diego good fun.

~ Travel Notes ~

Reservations needed for the Ghosts and Gravestones tour. Cost is $28 per person. Tours every evening at 6:30 except Tuesdays. Web site www.trolleytours.com

Take Interstate 5 south. Exit Front Street toward the Civic Center. Take the 2nd Ave. ramp. Merge onto Cedar St. Turn right onto 4th Ave. The tour starts at the corner of Island and 4th Ave. at the William Heath Davis House. A pay parking lot is located across the street.

The William Heath Davis House Museum at 410 Island Ave. is open for guided tours Tuesday-Friday 11 a.m. to 3 p.m. Weekends 10 a.m. to 4 p.m. Admission fee: $3 donation.

A self-guided walking tour available for purchase. Guided two-hour walking tours every Saturday at 11:00 a.m. Admission fee: $8

Horton Grand Hotel, 311 Island Ave. is across the street from the William Heath Davis House Museum.

Villa Montezuma is at 1925 K St and 20th Ave. Open Friday-Sunday 10 a.m. - 4:30 p.m. Admission fee: adults $5, kids 6-17, $2

In Old Town, the Whaley House Museum is in Old Town at 22482 San Diego Ave. Museum Open 10 a.m. – 4 p.m. year round, closed on Tuesdays. Admission fees: adults $5, seniors $4 and kids 3-12, $3.

El Campo Santo Cemetery is just a few blocks east also on San Diego Ave.

Victorian Ginger Nuts

Converting ingredient measurements given in pounds in this Victorian recipe proved a challenge. This cookie is firm and good for dipping.

2 cups flour
¼ pound butter
1 cup sugar
2 teaspoons ground ginger
1 cup light molasses
Warm water

Preheat oven to 350°.

By hand work chilled butter into flour. Continuing to work with hands, add sugar and ginger.

When well incorporated, add molasses gradually while stirring until mixture hold together. If still too crumbly add tablespoons of warm water until dough is stiff but can be formed.

On an oval tablespoon, heap and press with hands into a rounded nut-like form. Slip off spoon and if desired, dip tops in sugar before baking on greased baking sheet for 15-20 minutes until firm to the touch. Cool on rack.

Makes about 24.

Trail of The Presidio

Walk through Presidio Park in Old Town,
Fort Stockton Site and Father Serra Museum

$\maltese$

Gazpacho

High ground mesa and San Diego River-formed canyon.
For Spain, a good place to establish a military outpost
and a Mission on the Pacific Coast. For us, a rejuvenating walk
in a park through centuries of history.

On the TRAIL OF THE PRESIDIO we march single file
down a well-trodden path guarded by aromatic pines. Old
eucalyptus trees with restless unruly leaves and tall slender
Mexican Fanpalms form sentinels against the sky.

We wonder: how had these exotic trees and shrubs
shielding the lane, securing us in greenery, come to be here
and what happened to the drought-resistant plants and trees
that must have originally covered the mesa? It certainly
couldn't have looked like this lush paradise when Gaspar de
Portola's land party arrived in 1769. And what is that white
tower with sun glinting off it high above the steep canyon wall
before us? With these questions in mind we trod on.

Captain Gaspar de Portola

In 1768 Don Gaspar de Portola, a Catalonian of noble
birth and then Governor of Baja California, became
commander-in-chief of Spain's land and sea expeditions by
sailors, soldiers and missionaries with the goal of establishing
military outposts on the Pacific Coast.

The first outpost was established at the foot of Presidio
Hill where we walk. Eventually, Spain controlled Alta

41

California from four Presidios, the others strategically established in Santa Barbara, Monterey and San Francisco.

Neglected mature palms escort us down into the canyon. Mesmerized by our solitude, I bound up a neglected wooden stairway. "The stairs to nowhere," Dad says as I disappear and reappear after finding only a parking lot with a sign saying "no lewd acts in the Park." That snaps us out of our reverie and speaks of other uses the seclusion afforded. The path swings around a picnic arbor where fat squirrels wait for a handout.

On the dirt path we sometimes walk a golden carpet of minty eucalyptus leaves and sometimes slip and slide on a cover of oak leaves. We cross over the canyon and return up the other side.

Our circle route delivers us to an open velvet lawn. Dwarfed by a grove of lofty pine trees, we agree the Presidio Park is well-cared for. But it is not pampered.

Spanish soldiers who were called leather jackets, sailors, Franciscan missionaries from New Spain and Kumeyaay Indians once lived, worked and worshipped on this land. But in 1835, Spain lost control of the Presidio to Mexico. And in 1837 San Diego became a pueblo and the Hill was forgotten. Nothing visible remains of the settlement except buried adobe walls and some excavated artifacts.

Fort Stockton

Jasmine perfumes the air. A set of steps takes us to two eucalyptus trees, drooping leaves swooshing and swaying listlessly. Historical markers and memorials remind of the significance of the short-lived American military use of Presidio Hill. The plaque reads:

> *After American forces took old town during the Mexican War it was retaken and briefly held by Californios. It fell to the Americans once more who renamed it Fort Stockton and used it as campaign headquarters to end the California revolt of 1847. The Mormon Battalion stayed here later that year.*

The post was abandoned on September 25, 1848.

The roar of the Freeways encircling the Park fast forwards us into the twenty-first century. From this high ground we realize what made the hill so invaluable. Friend or foe advancing by land or by sea would be very visible, making it a formidable stronghold.

Father Serra Museum

We proceed up an embankment with other morning visitors to the Park to the Father Serra museum. It is closed today. A marker on the Serra Museum wall reads:

> *In memory of the founder of the California missions. On this hill, July 16, 1769 Padre Junipero Serra and soldiers of Spain set the royal standard raised the cross and dedicated Mission San Diego de Alcala.*

The white Spanish Colonial building we had seen from the canyon is not the original Mission but the Father Serra Museum dedicated in 1929. This causes visitors some confusion. In 1774, the original Mission San Diego de Alcala was relocated six miles inland in current day Mission Valley near the San Diego River.

We read on another wall the name of the man responsible for the preservation of this site. George White Marston changed the dry hillside to the lush jungle of Presidio Park.

Father Serra Museum

George White Marston

In 1907, George White
Marston dreamed a big dream
of preserving the site of the
first San Diego Mission. Over
the course of many years, he
bought up land and hired
landscape architect, John
Nolen, to design a plan for
groves of trees and to plant
thousands of shrubs and exotic
specimens from around the
world. Dedicated in 1929, the
plaque reads, "He presented
Presidio Park to the city he
loved as a memorial to Padre
Serra."

Strolling Presidio Park

The high ground formed by the river San Diego is a good
place to remember San Diego's past. And thanks to Marston,
a place to get off the beaten path of everyday life and be
renewed by a winding path to nowhere.

~ Travel Notes ~

From Interstate 5, exit Old Town Ave. and follow signs to
Old Town State Park. Just up the hill and east of Old Town is
the Serra Museum at 2727 Presidio Dr. in Presidio Park. Open
Friday, Saturday and Sunday from 10:00 to 4:30 Admission
fees: Adults $5, Children 6-17 $2.

To follow our Presidio Trail dirt path loop, start the Trail
by the restrooms under the stand of pine trees up the road
from the Serra Museum. This short easy Trail skirts the right
side of the canyon, crosses over and returns up the other side
and back to where you started. Look for the Fort Stockton site
sign on Presidio Drive nearby where the hike started.

There are picnic tables under an arbor along the Trail.

GAZPACHO

This is a simple version of a cold soup from Spain.

5 tomatoes, diced
3 cucumbers, peeled and diced
1 green pepper, chopped
1 red pepper, chopped
5 green onions, chopped
2 cloves garlic, minced
12-ounce can tomato or V8 juice
¼ can diced green chilies
3 tablespoons lime juice
1 tablespoon olive oil
2 tablespoons fresh parsley or cilantro, finely chopped
Salt and pepper to taste
Sour cream or green olives for garnish

Combine all ingredients except garnish in a 32-ounce container. Cover and refrigerate until thoroughly chilled.

Can be garnished with a dollop of sour cream or green olives. Serve in cups or bowls with spoons.

Serves 6.

Trail of the Birds

*Beach walk along Border Field State Park and visit to
Tijuana River National Estuarine Reserve Visitor Center,
Imperial Beach, San Diego*

ᚠ
Kalamata Olive and Tuna Tapenade Bruschette

I'll warn you up front. I have heard Border Field called the ugliest Park ever! No white slips of sand for sunning or dazzling blue ocean for swimming. In fact, swimming is not even recommended here and then there are those pesky helicopters. But beauty is in the eye of the beholder especially when it comes to Border Field. It may not be everyone's cup of tea but this wild chaotic bit of heaven at the beach is an international "Club Med" for birds.

On the TRAIL OF THE BIRDS, we exit Interstate 5 and find ourselves meandering along Dairy Mart Road. To the south we can see the well-traveled road leading out of Tijuana, Baja California ascending the reddish-brown terrace. Winding along Monument Road, we pass ranches and horse pastures. Fields gone wild with yellow daisies are in stark contrast to the manicured green lawns we have just left behind.

There is no politically correct way to say this. The helicopters circling here make it feel like a battlefield. They search for Mexican citizens and others illegally crossing the border into the United States. The helicopters seem at odds with the rare and endangered species of plants and birds now protected by the Park. Yet they are entangled here by politics, geography, environmentalism and historical events.

The road to Border Field throws us back in time to 1848 when the Treaty of Guadalupe Hidalgo ended the Mexican-

American War. The Mexicans called it the North American invasion of Mexico. After that treaty, the United States owned California and it became the first state on the coast of the Pacific Ocean. The estuary for the Tijuana River became the official dividing line between the United States and Mexico and it forms the southern boundary of the Park.

The Estuary

A watershed of rivers, streams and freshwater creeks flows over 1,700 square miles through Mexico, past Tecate and Tijuana and meets the Pacific Ocean tide here. An estuary is an inlet of the sea at the lower end of a river. This is one of two undiminished estuaries in southern California. It is essential to the existence of the Least Bell's Vireo, California Least Tern and Light-footed Clapper Rail, to name a few of the endangered and threatened species of birds that live in the Reserve.

Border Field State Park

Dad parks the car and we walk to the Park. A few yards down the road, a family of six startles us. In a dash across our path in a chain of clasped hands, they glance sideways at us and without skipping a step, sprint across the border from Mexico into the United States. We realize we are the only early morning park visitors not moving under the cover of Coastal Sage Scrub. Determined to go ahead with the plan to run through the Park and cross the Tijuana River to Imperial Beach, Mom and I investigate farther down the sandy lane. Dad returns to the car.

Arrows point the way to equestrian and walking trails. Picnic tables and a horse corral stand empty. Choppers circle to the north, taking off and landing at the field up the coast. Mom decides against walking farther and hikes back to the car, a glimmer in the sun.

The Tijuana River

Wondering if fording the river is possible, I begin the run. We have agreed to rendezvous in about an hour at the Imperial Beach Pier. The trail runs through the green Coastal Sage Scrub and is a soft tawny path that leads me to the ocean. In the cloudless blue sky, two russet-brown birds fly ahead on blue-gray wings. They seem to summon me past the salt flats and marsh toward the final mile of California beach. Abruptly they turn and wheel south toward the bullring stadium in Tijuana, Baja California.

I take this to be a good omen and inhale the salty air. At my feet the white brackish earth painted with tiny orange plants reveals a dynamic habitat flushed by tides.

The San Diego Formation

Soon I reach the beach. The waves toss at angles to the shore in crescendos of frothy white water. Two to three million years ago the Pacific Ocean claimed six to ten miles more of what is now San Diego and the Baja peninsula. Rivers carried sand and rock from the land and then dropped this debris into the ancient ocean. This yellowish sediment eventually formed what geologists call the San Diego Formation. About 500,000 to a million years ago faulting raised this Formation and created hilly landforms along the coast. Over time, waves eroded the landforms into a plain edged by the ocean. Geologists call this wave-cut bench the Lindavista Terrace. As I look back at the mesa behind me in Mexico, the flat-topped hills now illustrate the powerful forces at work along the coast.

A Shower of Birds

Suddenly a shower of black and white unfamiliar birds with shallow forked tails greets me. They flap narrow wings and swoop close to my head. My human presence on the beach seems to interest them.

This beach vibrates with life and not just with the occasional seagull and sandpiper. Birds rule—I mean rule. The beach dunes that form when wind and wave action deposit sand are designated off limits from April to August for California Least Tern nesting. Prostrate dune plants with yellow flowers like Beach Evening Primrose and the vines of Sand Verbena help stabilize the dunes.

Marbled Godwits

A helicopter circles as I snap pictures of seven Marbled Godwits, long upturned bills poked into the sand, digging for crustaceans. They dance on legs built for walking the marshes and dodging the waves. I wish for legs like these now for crossing the Tijuana River, a brown obstacle of undeterminable depth flowing across the beach to the ocean before me.

Following the right bank of the river a short way inland, seeking a crossing that will not humiliate me, I reach higher ground. The river spreads out and hundreds of California Brown Pelicans rest on the other side, just where I want to be. Perhaps this is a rest stop for them on the way to feeding grounds out in the ocean. The helicopter with whirling blades flushes them and then disappears in search of interlopers.

The Crossing

Halfway between the ocean and the pelicans, I pull up my pant legs and walk into the cold river. I take one, two, three steps. By four, the water rises above my knees. I slide my feet along the sandy bottom and pray I won't step into a hole and plunge into the tea-colored water. Counting to keep focused, I move forward. Five, six, seven-I am up to my hips. I hold the camera high. Preparing to go deeper, I brace for a strong current. There is none. Forty-two, forty-three steps taken, I finally emerge on the other side. Elated and triumphant, I trot ahead onto Imperial Beach. Here, birds rule no more. But surfers do!

Imperial Beach Pier

They group outside the waves and wait for the perfect set. Point Loma is a foggy vision in the distance.

Mom and Dad arrive at the Pier, glad to see I made it across. A ground squirrel had entertained them back at Border Field. I change out of my soggy clothing and jump into the car.

Tijuana River National Estuarine Reserve Visitor Center

The Visitor Center for the Tijuana River Estuary Reserve, which includes Border Field, is awash with the bright yellow faces of the Bush Sunflower. Outside of the simple but elegant building with its glass steeple, we examine local native coastal plants. I point out several favorite good smelling plants identified as Cleveland Sage and Black Sage.

Tijuana River National Estuarine Reserve

Bird Demonstrations

Inside the Center we manipulate puppets representing birds to show how their unique beaks reflect where they feed. I discover the birds that flew so buoyantly overhead at Border Field are California Least Terns, a member of the gull family. Their nests are but a scrape in the sand and a few sticks. No longer hunted for feathers, they still lack undisturbed beach for nesting. The good omen birds were kestrels, one of the most common southern California falcons.

The Marsh Trails

Outside on the walking trails, an excited man asks us, "Do you have binoculars?" Pointing to where he had just spotted an American Avocet, he tells us, "You will know it by its distinctive *kleet-kleet* voice."

Sure enough, as soon as we approach its territory, the unfamiliar creature buzzes overhead, with an alarmed *kleet-kleet*. The black and white bird flies gracefully, lovely legs dangling and long bill curved upward. As we leave the reserve, the avocet gives us a good riddance, farewell *kleet*. It flies freely between Mexico and the United States. We feel delight in meeting a visiting avocet and investigating its summer marsh.

It makes us wonder if the family we ran into made it across the border. Hopes of opportunity in America and dreams of those who would protect our vanishing estuaries somehow coexist here. Now I call that beautiful!

View south to Mexico

~ Travel Notes ~

To reach Border Field exit Interstate 5 on Dairy Mart Road and turn right. At 2 miles Dairy Mart Rd. becomes Monument Rd. Proceed 2 more miles, passing a Border Field sign. There are picnic tables at the park entrance. Trail access is flat and easy. Good for running or walking. Bring a pair of old shoes and binoculars. The easiest time to cross the river is at low tide. (*not recommended for small children.*) Swimming in the ocean off Border Field is also not recommended. Respect the dune closure and do not trespass beyond special area closure signs. *Do not walk into Mexico.*

The park opens irregularly depending on conditions and the season. On our next visit, winter rains had completely washed out the last section of road making it impassable by car.

The Tijuana Estuary Visitor Center is at 301 Caspian Way off 3rd Street. (3rd Street becomes Imperial Beach Blvd.) in Imperial Beach. From Interstate 5, exit at Coronado Ave. exit, turn right. Go west to 3rd St. and turn left at the stop sign. Follow 3rd St. to Caspian Way.

From Coronado take Highway 75 south to Rainbow Dr., turn right. Turn right on Palm Ave. Turn left on 3rd St. to Caspian way.

Visitor Center is open 7 days a week. Picnic tables are available. The reserve walking trails are open every day one-half hour before sunrise to one-half hour after sunset.

After exiting Visitor Center, take a left on Seacoast Dr. Proceed to the end of the road for a view of the estuary, the dunes and the ocean.

Kalamata Olive and Tuna Tapenade Bruschette

1½ cups brine cured Kalamata black olives, rinsed and drained
2 tablespoons capers, rinsed and drained
2 tablespoons olive oil
1 teaspoon lemon juice
Pinch cayenne pepper
2 garlic cloves, minced
2 anchovy fillets, rinsed and drained
½ cup chunk light tuna in oil, drained

Rinse and pat olives dry. To remove pits place olives on cutting board, press down firmly with a flat knife and roll slightly to split. Discard pits.

Rinse capers and anchovies in cold water, pat dry. In a food processor, puree anchovies and capers first. Add olives, olive oil, lemon juice, cayenne pepper, garlic cloves and drained tuna. Puree well.

Place in portable container and refrigerate. Serve on bruschette.

Serves 6.

Bruschette

Cut one baguette of Italian or French bread into ½-inch slices. Toast under the broiler until golden brown on both sides. Rub one side with garlic clove and brush same side with extra-virgin olive oil. Cool completely.

Place in airtight container. These can be made up to one week in advance.

Trail of the Silver Strand

*Run Beach Preserve, skate Silver Strand State Beach
and Crown Cove, Coronado*

Ŧ

Mahi Mahi Grilled Sandwich
Crown Cove Crunchy Coleslaw
Grilled Grunion
Grilled Green Onions

The shallow milky-blue waters of San Diego Bay lap on the east side of Silver Strand. The deeper clearer waters of the Pacific Ocean break on the west side. Beachgoers decorate the sand with colorful umbrellas. They flock to the improved portion of the beach boasting parking for a thousand cars and recreational vehicles. But the crowds thin farther down the coast where the Natural Beach Preserve attracts birds and beachcombers.

On the TRAIL OF THE SILVER STRAND, Mom and Dad walk beneath the highway through a tunnel to explore Crown Cove on the Bay. I go for a run along the Natural Beach Preserve section of Silver Strand Beach.

My feet sink into white sand glittering with sand dollars and cockleshells. No sea cliffs rise above this shore. The sand and the dunes here are part of what is called a Coastal Strand. Life is hard for plants in this environment. Survival on a beach dune may be as

Birds of Crown Cove

55

difficult as survival on a sand dune in the desert. Low-to-the-ground succulents with long taproots like Beach Sagewort and Dune Buckwheat found at the beach are related to desert plants.

Another phenomenon of this unique Strand is the California Grunion fish. This is not the season but at night in the spring and summer these sandy beaches attract this slippery silver fish. They arrive with the highest tides just after a full or new moon to lay eggs. People catch them with bare hands under a moonlit sky. They make for a delicious fish-fry but you do need a fishing license.

I step on seaweed that has washed ashore. A cloud of black kelp flies swarm up around my legs. I return to my starting point and pull on skates to explore the Crown Cove on the Bay side.

Skating to the Bay side is easy. Three pedestrian tunnels cross under Silver Strand Boulevard.

Crown Cove

On the Bay side at Crown Cove splashing waves replace crashing waves and breezes are less sharp. The crystal blue Bay is calm and warmer than the ocean for wading and swimming. Gray benches set along the beach encourage bird watching and that is where I find Mom and Dad laughing at a surf scooter tooting along against the current. One Snowy Egret picks and pokes the mudflat. My movements startle a flock of godwits. Usually seen in ones and twos, the flock flaps away in unison.

Crown Cove picnic area

Beach Grass

Purple Sea Fig and yellow Beach Primrose color the sand while serving an essential purpose. Fibrous roots hold the dunes steady while leaves and branches collect sand and keep it from blowing away.

Picnic tables under wooden ramadas and huge black cookers designate a group picnic area. A California Ground Squirrel complains indignantly at our intrusion. The paved path ends but one can follow on foot along the shore north to a boat landing and more beaches.

Bike Path

Once more I don trusty skates leaving Silver Strand behind and head out on the bike path paralleling the highway toward Imperial Beach. I wheel along the Bayshore bikeway past the South Bay Biologic Study area. Osprey and Belding's Savannah sparrow may be spotted in the small salt marsh. The waters of the San Diego Mountains flow together here in the robin's egg-blue Bay. In the distance, Otay Mountain is a gray specter above golden grasses. Reluctant to leave the home of native plants like glasswort and pickleweed, I fly across the Otay Marsh wetland past the cattails and bulrushes to the path's end in Imperial Beach where Dad's chariot awaits me.

L.M. Pepper Park

We sweep a few miles up the freeway, north to the Chula Vista Marina and Bayside Parks. A small place on the Bay's Sweetwater channel is called L.M. "Pep" Pepper Park. On the lawn, boys fly kites and people on lunch breaks picnic. We end our day watching ships unload cargo across the Bay.

~ Travel Notes ~

From Interstate 5 south, exit at Highway 75 and cross the Coronado Bridge. Silver Strand State Beach is 4.5 miles south of the city of Coronado on Highway 75. From Interstate 5 north, exit at Palm Avenue and go west on Highway 75. The Highway divides the ocean portion of the Park from the Bay side. Pedestrian tunnels run under the highway. From the Silver Strand parking area to the Otay River Marsh is approximately 5 miles one way.

Grills, fire rings and many ramada-shaded picnic tables are available at the Crown Cove picnic area. There are also fire rings for a bonfire. The paved bike path runs between San Diego Bay and the Pacific Ocean.

Crown Cove Crunchy Coleslaw

Use this as the topping for the sandwich.

4 teaspoons canola oil
6 tablespoons white wine vinegar
2 tablespoons sugar
2 teaspoons red onion, minced finely
2 teaspoons Dijon mustard
½ teaspoon caraway seeds
16 small chopped green olives with pimento
4 cups finely shredded green cabbage

In a small bowl mix together oil, vinegar, sugar, red onion, mustard, caraway seeds and green olives.

Add cabbage and toss well. Salt and pepper to taste.

Makes enough to top 4 sandwiches generously.

Mahi Mahi Grilled Sandwich

⅓ pound Mahi Mahi per person
Kaiser rolls
Mayonnaise

Have fish cut into individual servings. Spray cold grill and grill basket with cooking spray. Coat both sides of fish steaks with mayonnaise to keep moist.

When coals are medium hot cook fish about 10 minutes per inch of thickness, turning once. Fish is done when it is opaque and flaky. Toast buns lightly on the grill.

Serve with coleslaw on the sandwich.

Grilled Green Onions

Trim about 4 onions per person leaving several inches of green stem.

Place onions in a grill basket on medium-hot grill. Cook, turning frequently no longer than 5 minutes.

Grilled Grunion

If you are so lucky as to catch grunion in season, here is one way to cook them.

2½ pounds grunion
Salt
1 onion, chopped
Olive oil
Parsley, chopped
Lemons

Clean, wash and dry grunion. Sprinkle with salt.

Make 6 aluminum foil packets. Roll fish in olive oil and top with onions and parsley. Place in packets, sealing tightly.

Cook on medium hot grill for about 10 minutes until fish is flaky.

Serve with lemon.

Trail of Mission Bay

Skate and drive Mission Bay, San Diego

H

Campfire Tapas with dipping sauce
Dessert Tapas
California Sangria

I zero in on an unfamiliar large white bird in the marsh. A man with binoculars stands next to me on the platform. I ask, "What kind of bird do you think it is?" He cuts me off as if this is some kind of bad pick-up line.

"I have no idea. I'm here to watch the Thunder Boat drag races out in the Bay." Embarrassed, I hurry away wondering just what a Thunder Boat is anyway?

On the TRAIL OF MISSION BAY, we explore what were the mudflats, salt marshes, and tidal channels of the San Diego River. Juan Rodriquez Cabrillo labeled this delta of the river False Bay in 1542. Then, the vast marsh masqueraded as the entrance to San Diego Bay and confused sailors.

We, too, start confounded. Not that we thought we were in the wrong bay but not knowing how to see 27 miles of serpentine shoreline connected by miles and miles of stairways, steel bridges and cement sidewalks. Separated from the ocean by a spit of land, it is billed as the largest aquatic park on the West Coast. In 1944, after World War II,

Mission Bay shoreline

the dredging, draining and filling started. The 4,600-acre Park project created jobs and recreation.

The Park offers everything from water-skiing to water taxis along a myriad of bays, coves and celery-green lawns.

Bonita Cove

Bonita Cove is picnic heaven. Like a Caribbean island in the vast park it hosts many large group picnics. Intense competition between volleyball teams has participants scoring "kills" on the sand courts of the wide, white sandy beach. And over-the-line softball tournaments are battled out here every year.

Bonita Cove

Bayside Walk

The Bayside Walk starts just south of Bonita Cove and can be followed north to the white beaches of Santa Barbara, San Juan and Santa Clara Coves, ending at Sail Bay. By car, we wind around to Crown Point Shores.

Crown Point Shores

On the Crown Point Shores peninsula, the minty scent of eucalyptus trees mixes with the smell of brackish water. Several Marbled Godwits peck at the grass. Here some of the remaining wetland acres of Mission Bay are a sanctuary for endangered California Least Terns and Light-footed Clapper Rails. Clapper rails build an ingenious buoyant nest in the cord grass that is loosely attached so it simply floats when the tides move in and out.

I hear the roar of boat engines out in the Bay. A public loading dock for boats is near the wildlife preserve.

A View of Sea World

The next day we return and retrace my steps along Crown Point, the boardwalk up the steps of a staircase. The elevation here provides a view that captures the high rises of downtown San Diego. Before the park was built, residents claimed to be able to row to downtown at high tide and walk the mudflats at low tide to where Sea World is today. Sea World opened its tree-filled grounds and ever popular exhibits of whales, dolphins and seals almost forty years ago.

Riviera Shores

Skates roll down steps to the boat beaching and swimming areas of Riviera Shores and back to Sail Bay where the Catamaran Hotel exudes Polynesian flavor. Blazing along, I bump into Mom and Dad strolling the Bayside Walk at Toulon Street. Dad likes sidewalks and green grass. His feet don't have to touch the sand!

I never did figure out what kind of white bird I saw out in the marsh when I insulted the racing fan. But I did learn the Thunder Boat hydroplane races have been rocketing around the Mission Bay course since the mid 1960s. The course, described as one of the premier events on the Thunder Tour, reports it as "very fast." *Miss Budweiser* ran the 2.5-mile oval racecourse at a world-record lap speed of 172.1666 mph! Mission Bay does have a little something for everyone to enjoy.

~ Travel Notes ~

Because of the size of this park, there are many possible routes. One way to reach Mission Bay from Interstate 5 north or south, is to exit at Sea World Dr. (the south border of Park.)

To reach Bonita Cove proceed to 1000 West Mission Bay Drive at Mariners Way.

Crown Point Shores is off N. Mission Bay Drive at 3700 Crown Point Dr. on the east shore of the Crown Point peninsula.

Sea World is at 1720 South Shore road in Mission Bay. Admission fee charged.

There are fire rings, covered picnic tables and grills throughout the park. Check park regulations before bringing alcohol into the park.

Campfire Tapas

In Spain these are served as appetizers but here they are our
main course. Simply lay out ingredients for guests to arrange
on skewers.

1 sourdough baguette
Olive oil
Head of garlic
8 ounces Mozzarella cheese, cubed in 1-inch chunks
Mushrooms
Fresh oregano, sage or basil leaves
2 red bell peppers cut into 1½ inch squares

Cut sourdough baguette into slices. Brush slices with olive oil.
On skewers thread in this order: one slice bread, one inch
chunk mozzarella cheese, garlic clove, mushroom, one fresh
oregano, sage or basil leaf, one piece red bell pepper. Repeat
ending with a bread slice.

Grill over the campfire. Turn frequently until vegetables start
to char and cheese begins to melt. Remove skewers and place
on plates. Discard herb leaves. Serve with dipping sauce.

Serves 10-12.

Seafood variation:
Shrimp with artichoke hearts

Beef variations:
Summer sausage, cocktail franks, ham or bologna.

Cheese variations:
Muenster, Gouda, Parmesan or Brie.

Vegetable variations:
Maui, pearl or green onions or olives.

Mexican variation:
Use tortillas instead of baguettes, Monterey jack or cheddar
cheese, whole chilies and onions.

Italian variation:
pepperoni and Provolone cheese

Dipping Sauce for Tapas

4 tablespoons mayonnaise
1 clove minced garlic
1 teaspoon lemon juice
1 tablespoon olive oil
2 teaspoons prepared horseradish, optional

Blend mayonnaise, garlic, lemon juice and olive oil.
Horseradish can be added for a kick.

Dessert Tapas

For grilling choose firmer, less ripe fruits.

Fresh pineapple
Nectarines
Apricots
Mangoes
Bananas

1 tablespoon butter
2 tablespoons brown sugar

Cut pineapple and nectarines into cubes. Thread fruit on skewers. Grill over low heat.

Cut plums, apricots and mangoes in half. Remove pits. Place skin side down in a grill basket and cook until skins are slightly charred. Turn and cook several more minutes.

Slice bananas. Top with butter and sprinkle with brown sugar and cinnamon. Wrap in foil sprayed with cooking spray. Cook over low heat until bananas soften. If desired, serve over ice cream or frozen yogurt.

California Sangria

1 bottle (about 3 cups) light, fruity California Chenin Blanc
One 7-ounce bottle of sparkling water
5 ounces triple sec
2 cups of lemonade
1 fresh peach, washed and sliced
1 orange, washed, sliced and seeds removed
2 limes, washed, sliced and seeds removed
4 fresh mint sprigs
Strawberries for garnish

In a large plastic pitcher mix all ingredients except sparkling water. Allow to stand several hours refrigerated.

Just before serving add sparkling water and ice to the pitcher. Garnish with whole strawberry.

~ JOURNEY 10 ~

Trail of Nostalgia

*Skate the Strand from the Crystal Pier to
Mission Beach and Pacific Beach*

꙳

Coney Island Weenie Roast
Doughboys on a Stick
Shirley's Spice Cake
Irish Coffee

There is only one southern California hotel I can recommend right on the Pacific Ocean! Well, there really is only one hotel on the Pacific that can advertise, "Sleep over the ocean." The unearthly location over the combers renders the cottages as popular as the stretch of beach between Mission Beach and Pacific Beach.

We maneuver along the old west section of historic U.S.101, Mission Boulevard. Cars rush past closed bars and restaurants. Truck drivers deliver tonight's cold Miller Beer to back entrances.

On the TRAIL OF NOSTALGIA, our itinerary sweeps into motion at the landmark Crystal Pier in Pacific Beach where a grand blue and white arch brushes the gray sky above the ocean and invites us to explore what is beyond. Mom and Dad heed the beckon of this mysterious ocean gateway.

The Crystal Pier in Pacific Beach

The Strand from the Crystal Pier to Mission Bay

I peel off south, in-line skates turned to the promenade called the Strand. Retail and residential buildings squeeze right down to the sidewalk paralleling the beach. Shop keepers open doors, vacuum and turn "closed" signs to "open." The aroma of sweet donuts drifts from the coffee shop where locals read newspapers and drink strong black java. This cool, colorless morning, I'd like to stop for hot tea, but I keep rolling past souvenir shops where shell mobiles clack-clack and wind chimes ka-clink in the light breeze.

The trustworthy California sun finally disintegrates the dull white marine layer. Now the Strand's clapboard homes seem to smell of fresh paint and the peaceful Pacific reflects a newborn blue sky full of possibility. And what possibilities city makers envisioned to bring land buyers to this shoreline, once only a clean white canvas of sand.

Mission Beach

Who could resist a casino, roller rink and rollicking dance hall? If it were the early 1900s, I'd be on roller skates and would find a pier, bathhouse and tent city. John D. Spreckels of the San Francisco sugar family, lured real estate buyers to this beach with the Mission Beach Amusement Center. Popular at the turn-of-the-century were indoor saltwater swimming pools and roller coasters. They called the pool the Plunge, and the roller coaster the Giant Dipper. Both attractions are still open today. Two riders get into one car; the operator engages the coaster. It click-click-clicks up the track. The riders stretch arms above heads and scream on the drop down.

The Plunge

My first fall on skates in years happens in front of the historic Plunge. No harm done thanks to cushy kneepads, but my tape recorder sustains some damage. Things that attract the twenty-first century crowd haven't really changed all that

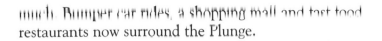

much. Bumper car rides, a shopping mall and fast food restaurants now surround the Plunge.

Mission Bay Entrance

At the entrance to Mission Bay, I run out of Strand. Turning back, I'm joined by other skaters and bikers along wide sun-spangled South Mission Beach. There is a momentum on wheels to this young-hearted town. Many worshippers of the sun bronze on blankets. Basketball players shoot hoops. And this is not a weekend; the Strand is the City of San Diego's most popular section of beach.

The Crystal Pier Hotel and Cottages

Back now at the Crystal Pier I spot Mom and Dad emerging from behind the grand arch. They describe the window-boxed, picket-fenced clapboard cottages lining both sides of the Pier.

The shops, arcades and ballroom built to entice land buyers in 1926 were later were remodeled to become the unique Crystal Pier Hotel & Cottages Motel, the only resort in southern California where you can "Sleep over the Ocean."

Sleep over the ocean

~ Travel Notes ~

To reach the Crystal Pier and Pacific Beach, exit at Grand Avenue off Interstate 5 and proceed to the end at the ocean. There are fire rings on the sand west of Ocean Blvd. in Pacific Beach. Crystal Pier web site: www.crystalpier.com

To reach Mission Beach at the center of the Strand, exit at Grand Avenue off Interstate 5 and proceed west to Mission Boulevard. Go left (south) on Mission Boulevard; look for the Giant Dipper roller coaster at West Mission Bay Drive.

To reach South Mission Beach, exit at Sea World Drive off Interstate 5. Look for directional signs to West Mission Bay Drive. Go left on Mission Boulevard, proceed to the south end of Mission Boulevard and turn right for public parking.

Coney Islands

A popular Coney Island hot dog restaurant in downtown St. Paul, Minnesota served a version of this old-time recipe for many years.

2 tablespoons butter
½ cup chopped onions
1 pound lean ground beef
1 teaspoon salt
2 teaspoons chili powder
1 cup catsup
2 teaspoons paprika
10-12 frankfurters and buns

Cook onions in butter until soft. Stir in meat, salt, paprika and chili powder. Cook over medium heat until meat is lightly browned. Blend in catsup and continue cooking 20 to 30 minutes. Add a little water to the mixture if too thick.

Pack in thermos for the beach.

For a Ruben style dog top with drained sauerkraut, strips of Swiss cheese and Thousand Island dressing.

Baguettes can be hollowed out and used for bun. Stuff with roasted hot dogs and condiments.

The weenie roast is the simplest campfire menu to prepare and with choices from basic dogs to gourmet sausages and mustards you can please everyone. Try bratwurst for an old fashioned taste. For kids another choice is to roast bologna on a stick and dip in mustard or ketchup. Build fire about 15 minutes before cooking. Bring skewers and plenty of napkins.

Doughboys

These take patience and time to cook slowly over the fire. Many drop into the fire and gave us all the giggles as everyone vied to make the best one. They were rated from awful to delicious depending on the skill of the doughboy cooker.

4 cups biscuit mix
1 cup water
Honey, jam, butter or chocolate chips
Flour for handling
Oven mitt or gloves
Wooden skewers or dowels soaked in water

Mix 4 cups biscuit mix with 1 cup water creating a dough.

With lightly floured hands, shape dough around end of skewers, making a hot dog bun shape about 4 inches long and ½-inch thick. Pinch ends together.

Toast over the fire for about 10 minutes until cooked through, twirling to keep even and from falling off the stick.

When done, remove and fill the hole left when the skewer is removed with honey, jam, butter or chocolate chips.

Serves 12.

Shirley's Spice Cake

2½ cups sifted flour
1 teaspoon baking powder
1 teaspoon baking soda
1 teaspoon salt
1 teaspoon cinnamon
½ teaspoon cloves
⅛ teaspoon pepper
½ cup soft butter
½ cup light brown sugar
1 cup granulated sugar
2 eggs
1 teaspoon vanilla
1¼ cups buttermilk

Preheat oven to 350°. Grease and flour a 13x9x2 inch-baking pan. Sift together flour, baking powder, soda, salt, cinnamon, cloves and pepper.

In large bowl of high-speed mixer beat butter, sugars, eggs and vanilla about 5 minutes. At low speed add in dry ingredients (in fourths) with buttermilk (in thirds) and beat until smooth, about 1 minute.

Pour in pan and bake 40-45 minutes. Frost as desired.

Irish Coffee

Thermos of hot coffee
Irish whiskey
3 brown sugar cubes per serving
Whipped cream

In a coffee mug, pour ½-inch Irish whiskey. Add brown sugar cubes. Leaving enough room to top with ½-inch whipped cream, fill cup with good hot coffee. Swizzle and top with whipped cream.

Trail of Isolation

Visit Windansea Beach, La Jolla

A

Parsley and Ham Sandwiches

The cliffs before me shape shift. To my eyes they become a mile-long yellow camel lying on its side. Light brown belly and flanks of sandstone form soft beaches below. These curving inlets and isolated coves inspired poets and a famous writer of the "beat generation."

On the TRAIL OF ISOLATION, our itinerary leads us into a neighborhood of elegant homes along the treelined boulevards of south La Jolla. Exploring the stairways, overlooks and small landscaped parks, we discover flat, wide sandy beaches have been left behind and we arrive at intimate pocket beaches and rocky points.

Bird Rock and Sun Gold Point

The name, Sun Gold Point, seems to reflect the light on the rocks and sand that sparkle along the sea. We stand out on the rocky point of Bird Rock to visualize the old Bird Rock Inn, constructed of beach stones. It is said that Charles Lindbergh dined at this Inn in the days prior to taking off for New York and Paris in the *Spirit of St. Louis*. The stone building gone, Bird Rock flyers are now California Brown Pelicans and sea gulls with a landing pattern of their own— white guano.

Windansea

The offshore reefs at Windansea generate world-class waves and these waves have attracted surfers as far back as the

1940s, when a legendary surf culture was spawned. These pioneers of the sport put up a thatched ramada hut, dubbed the "Shack." The rebuilt structure's palm fronds still provide shade.

Windandsea Hideaway

The Pumphouse Gang

Shelters of soft, rounded, wind and wave sculpted sandstone hide students. I stumble into their private kingdoms tucked along the warm rocks and outcroppings. Crystalline water laps at the soft rock. I sneak a peek at books to see if any one reads the writers that this beach stirred. Allen Ginsberg and Lawrence Ferlinghetti may have walked here before doing a poetry reading at the "Pour House." Unfortunately this nearby hangout, once located a few blocks east on La Jolla Boulevard, has gone the way of the Bird Rock Inn. Tom Wolfe immortalized the surfers who gathered here in his 1968 book, *The Pumphouse Gang*.

Epic Waves

The epic waves that drew this crowd break hard on the steep shore emphasizing why lifeguards and regulars hope the novice surfer will stay off the plunging breakers of Windansea. I discover what surfers know; waves are divided into three categories.

Plunging Breakers

A plunging breaker, a classic circular-backed wave with a hollowed-out front, has a crest that pitches in advance of the lower part of the wave. A surfer paddles hard to get his board going at a speed where the wave energy propels him forward as it rises up under the board. Once up on the face, he maneuvers sideways across the surface of the plunging breaker.

Spilling and Surging Breakers

If this beach sloped more gently and was not a shore break, the wave crest, mushy at the top, would just spill down the face in a cascade; it is thus named a spilling breaker. If the water offshore was very deep then the wave crest might take shape but flood onto the beach without spilling or breaking, thus a surging breaker.

Ocean Personality

The ocean is habitual, predictable and scholars say, even has a personality. If I had ocean personality, I'd want to be a spectacular plunging breaker! It occurs to me today that I'm just a note-taker and student like all the others along the Windansea shore. The ocean writes its own story.

The rising tide inching up into the sandstone nooks forces me into a retreat. I move south on a small footpath to walk the back of the "camel" alone. With not enough hideaways to go around in this world, it is good to find such a place and get wrapped in a golden moment in the sun, insulated from distraction, contemplating a Windansea wave and writers inspiration.

Legendary surf

~ Travel Notes ~

To reach Windansea Beach from Interstate 5, take La Jolla Village Drive exit and proceed west. Turn left on Torrey Pines Road. Follow Torrey Pines Road to Pearl Street and turn right. Turn left on La Jolla Boulevard. Turn right on Nautilus.

Beach access is easy. Best time to picnic is low tide. No facilities.

To reach Sun Gold Point and Bird Rock from Windansea Beach follow Camino de la Costa south along the coast approximately one mile to Sun Gold Point and another one-half mile to Bird Rock Avenue.

Parsley and Ham Sandwiches

⅛ cup fresh basil, finely chopped
¼ cup fresh parsley, finely chopped
1 cup low fat mayonnaise
1 large clove garlic, finely chopped
4 pimento stuffed olives, finely chopped
12 slices white bread, crusts removed
¼ pound ham thinly sliced
Butter

Chop and mix basil, parsley, garlic and olives. Add to mayonnaise. Cover and refrigerate at least 1 hour.

Coat each bread slice thinly with butter. Spread with mayonnaise mixture. Top with ham covering completely. Cover with second slice and press slightly to compact. Cut into 4 pieces.

Makes 24 squares.

Trail of Gifts of the Sea

Walk the La Jolla Cove and Bluffs

℞

Smoked Salmon Spread on Rye
Cold Dilled Shrimp

Park up on ritzy Prospect Street then stroll through the shops and peek into the courtyard of the pink Hotel La Valencia. Take a walk south and drop down a steep bend and sneak up on the Cove! The surprising splash of blue water cresting with white glassy foam calms like a deep exhale. La Jolla's wild creatures greet with clamoring barks as they haul themselves up onto warm brown rocks and nearby white patches of beach.

The TRAIL OF GIFTS OF THE SEA begins as we hang out over the railing of the half-moon-shaped sea wall and watch the Harbor Seals, disturbed in their sunning places, diving deep into tourmaline blue-green water. These long-time residents live twenty to twenty-five years; their entire lives are spent along the La Jolla coastline.

Casa Pool in La Jolla Cove

Harbor Seals at the Casa Pool

It is not known why these normally shy and reclusive creatures tolerate human activity here. But it is known that

79

they have been here on the shores and rocks at least as far back as when Frank T. Botsford proclaimed it "magnificent" and bought over 400 acres of La Jolla Park in the late 1800s.

The American Riviera

Called the "American Riviera," La Jolla attracted many wealthy retirees. Turn-of-the-century travel writers compared a trip to southern California as akin to visiting a great European spa. Health seekers could try exotic, round fruits called oranges, bathe in the saltwater plunges and enjoy the tumbles of bougainvillea and desert flowers. This illusion of a strange and fascinating place spurred a fledgling tourist industry. The climate with dry summers and mild rainy winters, similar to lands bordering the Mediterranean Sea, added to the attraction. One dollar could buy a train ticket to paradise from the Midwest.

Often these blue-sky claims were greatly exaggerated. But it is safe to say, even now, La Jolla is on par with any destination on the Mediterranean.

Ellen Scripps Park

We cross the broad lawn of Ellen Scripps Park, named for one of the city's most influential women. Ellen Browning Scripps settled into town in 1887, already a self-made, wealthy woman. With a head for figures, she had wisely invested in her brother's venture, the *Detroit Evening News* and later other newspapers. As her wealth grew she still lived frugally and set aside money "for the benefit of humanity."

Three years after her retirement to La Jolla, brother George Scripps willed her an estate. Her background as a teacher led her into philanthropy and money flowed to schools, colleges and the YMCA. Hospitals and churches received donations. Her indelible mark can be seen in the institutions associated with La Jolla and San Diego: Scripps Memorial Hospital, Scripps Institute of Oceanography and the Natural History Museum and Zoological Garden at Balboa Park.

She also contributed generously to preserving La Jolla's natural "magnificence" with many gifts of land. The Casa Pool and sea wall, donated after several children were swept out to sea by deadly riptides there, connects us to her generosity today.

Coast Walk

We are drawn up the hill toward the Coast Walk. Goldfish Point protrudes out into the water and garibaldi fish swim nearby attracting many black-suited divers and snorkel-masked swimmers.

Native Americans trod these same coast bluffs. More than 10,000 years ago, nomadic tribes migrating to the coast chose La Jolla as one of their eight permanent settlements.

La Jolla Caves

Seven secret caves carve into sandstone cliffs and show the force of water. Mom and Dad slip away checking out the inviting restaurants and shops on the other side of the street. I enter a building and pay to descend over 100 slippery steps into the mouth of one of La Jolla's largest sea caves.

The cool cavity with slippery wet stone has the earthy aroma of a damp Midwestern basement. At the bottom of the steps waves break flooding into the cave. The dark cave is illuminated by the sunlight filtering into the cavern's mouth chiseled in the sandstone. It resembles a yawning silhouette of a man's face. This countenance gives the cave its nickname, "Sunny

Sunny Jim Cave

Jim." Saying goodbye to old Jim, I exit and return into La Jolla's brilliance.

Exploring farther along the bluff on the dirt trail, I sit down on an empty bench to watch an artist paint lipstick-red poppies on a white canvas. I survey the Cove and silently thank Ellen Scripps for her generous heart so instrumental in preserving La Jolla's gifts of the sea.

~ Travel Notes ~

To reach the La Jolla Cove area from Interstate 5 south, exit La Jolla Village Drive and go right. Turn left onto Torrey Pines Rd. Turn right onto Prospect Place. Prospect Place becomes Prospect Street. Turn right onto Girard Avenue. Turn left onto Coast Boulevard.

From Interstate 5 north, exit Ardath Road. Turn slight left onto Torrey Pines Road. Turn right onto Prospect Place. Prospect Place becomes Prospect Street. Turn right onto Girard Avenue. Turn left onto Coast Boulevard.

The La Valencia Hotel and restaurant is at 1132 Prospect Street. The Casa (Children's Pool) is at 850 Coast Boulevard. Ellen Scripps Park is at Coast Blvd. and Girard Avenue. Grass picnic area has fire pits. Coast Boulevard Park has picnic tables and thatched palapas.

La Jolla Cove is at 1100 Coast Boulevard. The Coast Walk dirt path can be found at Torrey Pines Road east of Prospect Street or from Goldfish Point area near Sunny Jim Cave at 1325 Coast Boulevard. Enter cave through shop.

Smoked Salmon Spread

Spread can be made up to 3 days in advance and placed in a cooler

8 ounces boned and skinned smoked trout or salmon fillets
Two 3-ounce packages reduced fat cream cheese
1 tablespoon each of prepared horseradish and fresh lemon juice
4 green onions, thinly sliced green and white parts
1 tablespoon fresh dill, minced
Party rye, pumpernickel bread or Granny Smith apples

Place smoked trout fillets in a medium bowl and flake with a fork. In another bowl soften cream cheese with 1 tablespoon each of prepared horseradish and fresh lemon juice. Combine with the fish and add green onion and fresh dill. Refrigerate until serving. Pack in cooler with a small knife and serve on party rye, crackers or apples.

Cold Dilled Shrimp

1 pound medium peeled and deveined shrimp
4 lemon slices

Marinade for shrimp:
1 lemon cut into 8 slices
1 cup water
¼ cup tarragon vinegar
¼ cup rice wine vinegar
⅓ cup minced fresh dill
3 chopped green onions
4 chopped inner celery ribs

Bring to a boil in a saucepan, shrimp, 4 lemon slices and water to cover. Reduce heat and simmer about 3 minutes until shrimp are cooked. If you are using already cooked shrimp rinse. Drain shrimp. Place in marinade of lemon slices, water, tarragon vinegar, rice wine vinegar, dill, green onions and celery ribs. Marinate overnight. Drain. Season with salt and pepper to taste. Pack for picnic in sealed container. Serve with toothpicks. Serves 4.

Trail of Cathedral Cliffs

Torrey Pines City Park, Burro Trail down to Black's Beach, beach
walk to La Jolla Shores Beach-Kellogg Park, La Jolla

ᛘ

Spicy Bouillon
Grilled Herbed Cornish Hens
Fresh Cranberry Sauce
Grilled Fresh Peaches
Cathedral Coffee

Cathedral cliffs like misplaced church walls of a sanctuary
soar high into the sky. Like a fortress above the ocean,
they appear solid and stable. I touch the fortification with a
finger. It crumbles. These golden cathedral walls are nothing
but layer upon layer of ancient sand. And not only are they
soft, these walls are silently sliding into the sea. Silently, except
for the thud when a chunk breaks off and plunges to the base
of the nearly vertical wall.

On the TRAIL OF CATHEDRAL CLIFFS, our itinerary
takes us to the glider port at the southeast corner of the Torrey
Pines City Park. My partners drop me off and drive down the
coast several miles south to meet me later at the Scripps Pier.

I stand atop the cathedral and watch the first hang glider
of the morning rush to the edge and jump. He trusts the
invisible updrafts to keep him from splattering down onto
infamous Black's Beach, 350 feet below. I take my chances on
the rugged Burro Trail to get down to the beach.

Burro Trail

The steep trail damaged by spring rains is washed out but
passable. Young, hard-body surfers, boards under arms, are
already climbing back up the trail. Fresh from a dawn patrol-
surfing session, they are fit, tan, dripping wet and looking as

85

peaceful as if Pacific Ocean saltwater runs through their veins.

I catch up with two sundried, longtime naturists and a young couple with white towels clutched in their hands. All will be clothing optional soon.

Clothing Optional

Once the only legal nude beach in southern California, Black's has not been clothing optional since 1977 but the practice still continues. Finally navigating the last slippy-slide portion of the trail, I drop down to the beach and rocket south on flying feet.

Unstable Cliffs

Down on the beach looking up, the magnificent cliffs absolutely go through the roof of the sky. But they have deceived the unsuspecting traveler. Occasionally a piece dislodges and plunges to the beach. Not long ago, two unlucky people were killed by falling debris.

Black's Beach

I have yet to see any nude sunbathers. I remember the snickers about Black's Beach when I was just a teenager visiting California in the 1980s. Today, I'm glad it is only surfers standing on the shore and not ogling tourists like my cousins who stripped here and burned their lily-white skin to a medium rare.

More surfers scramble down a paved trail at the south end of Blackgold Road and struggle into black wetsuits while others do requisite stretching exercises on the beach.

Submarine Canyon

What makes the surfing good here, other than potential nude surfing, is the convergence of two underwater submarine canyons. They form a valley on the sea floor and create big waves for the University of San Diego students lucky enough to have a campus on the plateau above the beach. With its foam running down the face of the cliff, the UFO-shaped structure on the shore is the National Marine Fisheries building.

Scripps Pier

As planned, my parents appear on the beach near the Scripps Pier. Dad reports some bad luck, a nail jammed into his tire.

Flat fixed, Dad drives to our lunch destination with a change of clothes for me; Mom joins me on the flat expanse of La Jolla Shores, near Kellogg Park. Florence Scripps donated the park as a memorial to her husband William Kellogg, another legacy of the philanthropic family.

La Jolla Shores-Kellogg Park

The beach is perfect for a stroll and popular with families for swimming. Stingrays swish their tails near shore. Shuffling the feet when entering the water is recommended to avoid contact.

I push on ahead and find the Marine Room Restaurant door and turn to signal Mom, a fashionable beachcomber holding onto her tan sunhat.

La Jolla Shores Beach

The Marine Room

Seated inside, with surf rolling almost up to the walls, we relax. Once more, like the cliffs there is a feeling of permanence but in the 1940s and again in 1980s, the Marine Room suffered significant storm damage.

Today, the earthen cathedral cliffs have lent a perception of an enduring world. But their stability is an illusion. When the occasional stone falls from the great heights of the seemingly solid cliff it gradually becomes only a polished grain of sand inevitably joining the sea.

~ Travel Notes ~

To reach Torrey Pines City Park Glider Port area, exit Interstate 5 on Genesee Avenue and go west. Turn left on North Torrey Pines Scenic Drive. Turn right at Torrey Pines Scenic Drive. Turn right at sign "Torrey Pines Glider Park." At the end of Torrey Pines Scenic Drive, follow dirt road to the parking area on left. Those needing easier access follow directions to La Jolla Shores below and walk north 1 mile.

To reach La Jolla Shores Beach-Kellogg Park from the south, exit Interstate 5 at Ardath Road. Turn right at La Jolla Shores Drive, and left at Avenida del la Playa. Turn right on Camino Del Oro. From the north, exit Interstate 5 at La Jolla Village Drive and go west. Turn left at Torrey Pines Road and follow to La Jolla Shores Dr.

Low tide is best for walking. There are grills, fire rings and picnic tables.

Award-winning Marine Room restaurant is on the beach at La Jolla Shores. From La Jolla Shores Drive head toward the ocean on Paseo Dorado and follow past golf course to restaurant on right.

Grilled Herbed Cornish Game Hens

The game hens are partially cooked in the microwave to speed up cooking time at the beach.

4 Cornish game hens split lengthwise
1 lemon
2 tablespoons olive oil
1 tablespoon chopped fresh thyme or 1 teaspoon dried thyme or basil
Mango chutney for garnish

Choose 4 Cornish game hens (about 2 pounds each) cut in half lengthwise, (butcher will cut for you) defrosted or fresh.) It will take about a day to defrost in refrigerator and can be kept thawed up to 3 days. Rinse and pat dry.

For a crisp skin and citrus flavor rub hens with a cut lemon. Place hens, breast side up, in a 2-quart casserole. Cover with microwavable cover and cook on high for 8 minutes. Change position of birds, cover again and cook on high for 8 more minutes. Refrigerate hens.

In a small container blend olive oil and herbs.

Place hens skin side down on a medium hot grill. Cook about 6 minutes. Turn hens over and baste with herb mixture. Cook about 6 more minutes until browned and juice run clear. Have a squirt bottle of water on hand for flare-ups.

Serve over a bed of field greens with light vinaigrette. Garnish with mango chutney. Serves 4.

Fresh Cranberry Sauce

4 cups fresh cranberries
2 cups sugar
2 cups water

Wash and pick over cranberries. Bring water and sugar to a boil in medium saucepan. Boil 5 minutes. Add cranberries and cover. Simmer gently until berries begin to pop. Chill. Makes 4 cups.

Mom's Spicy Bouillon

32 ounces tomato juice
4 bouillon cubes or 4 teaspoons Better Than Bouillon
1 cup water
½ bay leaf
1 tablespoon sugar
1 teaspoon each garlic salt and salt
½ teaspoon black pepper
¼ teaspoon cloves
1 tablespoon Worcestershire sauce
4 tablespoons fresh lemon juice
1 tablespoon minced parsley
1 stalk of celery, halved

In a saucepan combine all ingredients. Heat until boiling, turn heat down and simmer for 15 minutes. Remove celery stock.

Pack in thermos for beach. Serve hot.

Grilled Fresh Peaches

4 firm peaches
1 teaspoon cinnamon
⅓ cup sugar

Peel peaches. Roll in a mixture of cinnamon and sugar. Make aluminum foil packets sprinkling extra sugar mixture on top. Tightly seal.

Place around edges of grill and cook 10 minutes or until heated through. Serve in a bowl.

Cathedral Coffee

1½ ounces per serving ouzo (an anise-flavored liqueur of Greece)
½ ounce metaxa per serving (a Greek brandy)
1 teaspoon brown sugar per serving
1 cup strong American coffee per serving
Whipped cream
Licorice stick or straw

Pour into hot cup or mug starting with liqueurs and sugar. Top with float of whipped cream. Add straw or hollow stick of licorice for sipping.

Trail of a Rare Pine Tree

Walk along the Guy Fleming Trail and run Beach Trails,
Torrey Pines State Reserve and visit Sea Grove Park
and downtown Del Mar

A

Cucumbers and Sour Cream served in Pita Bread

A search for a rare native conifer draws us along the Guy
Fleming Trail in Torrey Pines State Reserve. Thorny
chaparral embraces the delicate tracings of wild snapdragons
and shooting star flowers. Mom trots behind me, slows, and
then stops. She yells down the trail to me, "Might be
rattlesnakes! I'm going back." I laugh having heard this before
in our desert adventures. The salty tang of ocean air turns to a
heavenly scent of pine.

On the TRAIL OF A RARE PINE TREE, I am soon face
to face with a relic of the Ice Age. The spreading green crowns
of Torrey Pine trees provide a small canopy of shade for me.
These native conifers are very rare and exist only here and on
Santa Rosa Island off the coast of California.

Punta de Los Arboles

When Spanish explorers first sighted these wooded
headlands over four hundred centuries ago, they named them
Punta de los Arboles, Point of Trees. Roots cling to an
extraordinary habitat here, coveted by humans for its tall cliffs,
sweeping surreal blue water and chaparral-covered mesas.

A collaboration of botanists and park planners created the
Torrey Pines State Reserve, just south of the city of Del Mar.
Ellen Browning Scripps acquired adjacent groves for the city
adding to acreage already set aside as a park. The Reserve now

includes the Los Penasquitos Marsh and Lagoon and upland Reserve Extension.

Torrey Pine Blue

On the precipice of a sheer cliff I gasp, wishing Mom had continued on to witness this sight! Far below me the ocean swirls. Crystal clear combers play in shades as rich as the wings of the blue jay I had seen on the trail. Delighted, I skip along musing about the ocean's color. Then it dawned on me. What I witness here is a one of a kind landscape repeated nowhere else on the coast. This ocean reflects this particular sky colored by the Torrey pine habitat that exists only here. It is Torrey Pine blue.

Ancient Bluffs

The ancient bluffs under my feet began forming about forty-five to fifty million years ago. A newer, rounded Bay Point body of rock forms the top. The middle formation is a honey-colored Torrey Sandstone. The Del Mar Formation makes up the bottom layer, peppered with prehistoric oysters, clams and snails. The three stacked layers look like spun gold.

A towering wall of sandstone, rilled and gullied by relentless wind, takes me by surprise when I orbit around the loop trail. Comparing notes at the end of the trail, Mom reports watching the same blue jay with wings the color of the ocean but no rattlers. We head to downtown Del Mar for another special treat.

Downtown Del Mar

This could be the French Riviera. Seated outside, shaded under market umbrellas, one is immediately relaxed at the posh Pacifica Del Mar restaurant. Looking out at the expansive panoramic view of the ocean, our thoughts turn to the beginning of this town.

A land boom was created on the coast in the 1880's when T.M.Loop promoted the building of a village here. It is said that Mrs. Loop, inspired by a poem, Paso del Mar, named their vision of a literary and artistic hamlet, Del Mar.

In the late 1930s, horse racing drew Hollywood celebrities Bing Crosby and Desi Arnaz to town bringing glamour, prestige and money. At the Del Mar Race Track, with its buildings in the elegant style of Spain, horses still shoot out of the starting gate to win, place or show in midsummer.

Sea Grove Park

After lunch we stroll two blocks to Sea Grove Park where sea lavender edges freshly mown grass. We rest in the shade of tropical bamboo; the sun warms our backs. I now recognize several of the Park's shade trees as Torrey Pines. On the terraced cliff below, a train from the nearby Amtrak station whizzes by on the way to San Diego.

We leave the understated elegance of Del Mar thankful for the rich opulence of this rare tree habitat preserved by visionaries of another century when open coastal land was still abundant.

Sea Grove Park, Del Mar

Torrey Pines Reserve, running the Beach Trail

Early on a July morning, I urge T.M. to see the Reserve I had been raving about. Starting close to the Adobe Visitor center and native plant gardens, we run the Beach Trail. It is three-quarters of a mile down the cliff to Flat Rock, a landmark on the beach below. Sandy switchbacks descend into a canyon fanning out with badland slopes across a desert-like landscape. A scattered few Torrey Pines rise above the abundant buckwheat and evergreen Lemonadeberry bushes. These berries are relished by roadrunners. Sweet pungent aromas are released in the warm sunlight. Swiftly, T.M. disappears into the narrowing canyon that drops us precariously to the beach.

South on the Beach

Down on the beach, south of Flat Rock, the tide is just low enough to pass without getting wet. Waves lash the cliffs hollowing out sea caves. When touched with a finger, the sandstone cliff crumbles. Initials carved on the soft wall speak to the thoughtlessness of some people. A turn back at Black's Beach returns us up the Broken Hill Trail and eventually connects to a section of historic US 101 and back to where we began.

Torrey Pines Reserve, the Beach Trail north

On another visit we trot down into the brooding still-shadowed canyon. At this early morning hour in October, the first creeping rays of sunlight sweep away the gloom and color the buckwheat plants into tiny golden Christmas trees. The Beach Trail advances us north. Though the high tide has been retreating for more than two hours, there is barely enough beach under our feet to pass. The ebb tide reveals fingers of green and brown stone. Black grains of sand mix with the white.

Penasquitos Marsh Natural Preserve

Brown pelicans plummet into the surf line and signal our approach to the Los Penasquitos Lagoon. Sand dunes and the Torrey Pines State Beach separate the lagoon from the ocean. At the Penasquitos Marsh Natural Preserve, the endangered Clapper Rail and Least Tern survive.

Godwits and sanderlings do a double quickstep on the wet sand. A lone Snowy Plover shows off his curved beak and striped eye while dodging waves. Three sandpipers obey the ebb and flow of the water in a practiced intertidal dance. Our steps are clumsy zigzags in the sand. We return, a bit tired but renewed in spirit by the birds and the open gold cliffs along this wild stretch of San Diego beach.

~ Travel Notes ~

The Torrey Pines State Reserve is between La Jolla and Del Mar. From Interstate 5 north or south, exit Carmel Valley Road and go west approximately 1.5 miles to Coast Highway 101. Turn left and drive along the beach for about 1 mile. Park entrance is on the right (before the road climbs up the steep grade.) Open daily from 8 a.m. until sunset. The Visitor Center on the bluff-top opens at 9 a.m. Web site: www.torreypine.org

Guy Fleming Trail is an easy two-thirds mile loop. Parry Grove Trail is a moderately difficult one-half mile loop. The steeper Beach Trail starts at restroom area and is a ?-mile trail to the beach at Flat Rock. Walking the beach is best at low tide and may be impassable under certain high tide conditions.

Picnicking and food are not allowed in the bluff-top Reserve. Food is allowed only to be carried to the beach. The Los Penasquitos Lagoon has picnic tables and on the beach side, Torrey Pines State Beach has a few tables.

Cucumbers in Sour Cream served in Pita Bread

This is an old family recipe with cucumbers sliced on a grandfather's handmade wooden vegetable slicer.

4-5 medium slender cucumbers
6 ounces sour cream
¼ cup rice vinegar
2 cloves garlic, finely minced
1-2 tablespoons sugar, to taste
Salt, to taste

Mix together in a small bowl sour cream, rice vinegar, garlic, sugar and salt to taste.

Peel medium slender cucumbers and slice very thinly into a medium size bowl. Can be done with a knife or slicer. Lightly salt each cucumber layer as you go. Place a dish smaller than bowl on top on the cucumbers and weigh down to draw out liquid. Let stand about 15-30 minutes.

Remove weighted cover and squeeze remaining liquid from cucumbers with hands. Discard liquid. Combine cucumbers with sour cream mixture. Allow to stand refrigerated for a least one hour. Slice pita bread in half and spoon cucumber mixture inside.

Trail of Tides

Walk the staircases and beaches of Encinitas.
Leucadia and Solana Beach

Ħ
Tandori Chicken Legs
Tabbouleh with Romaine Scoops and Fresh Mango

The rising tide swallows up a concrete boat launch ramp on the beach. Each rush of wave throws cobblestones up the ramp. Each drag of the wave scrapes them down hard against the metal handrailings with a violent clank-clank-clank. The rocks drop back into the sea, a not so subtle reminder of the dynamic ocean's power to rip away manmade static structures like tinker toys and reclaim the shore for her own.

Fletcher's Cove, Solana Beach

It is January, one of the three winter months along the California coast when the highest astronomical tides occur. With these higher than average tides coinciding with wind-driven surf, trouble may be brewing on the TRAIL OF THE TIDES.

The first of a series of winter storms stacked up off the Pacific Coast has just blown through San Diego in a fury of lightning strikes and a gushing downpour. Now between storms, storm watchers gather on a metal platform perched above Fletcher Cove in Solana Beach. The water churns in a muddied blue-green sea overlaid with boiling whitecaps.

Fletcher Cove

High tide combined with big waves has attracted this small crowd transfixed by the power of the heaving sea. Our stomachs tighten watching one lone surfer tossed about while attempting to paddle back to shore.

Magnificent explosions of white water break on the face of a dominant yellow cliff. "This is some angry ocean," Dad declares. A breaker splashes Mom and she retreats to the back of the platform. The ocean laughs at us in the booming echoes of the waves. They are as deceptive as a cat's paw curled and ready to strike. And strike they do over and over, spewing a salty mist pulsing with spent energy.

Rogue Wave Danger

Perched on our safe haven, we cling to a false sense of security. Finally the waves release the surfer. We breathe a sigh of relief as he climbs up to the platform. Then a young woman pushes a double

Big waves breaking on Fletcher Cove cliffs

stroller up the ramp and sets two toddlers free on the small slippery surface. An older man moves close to them, keeping a keen grandfatherly eye on the gap in the bottom of the railing where there is plenty of room for the tots to be swept away by a rogue wave. The girl seems unaware of any danger.

Tides

The night before a full moon glinted into our windows. This cosmic event has contributed to the high tide today as well as gravity and centrifugal force. Very simply put, the moon's gravitational pull on the earth combined with centrifugal forces causes a water bulge on the side of the earth closest to the moon and on the side farthest from the moon.

On the Pacific Coast, four mixed tides occur every 24 hours and 50 minutes, two different high tides and two varying low tides.

Spring Tides

Although the sun's influence on the tides is less than that of the closer moon, the water bulges do become larger when the sun, moon and earth are in a straight line during a full moon and a new moon. These tides of greater variation are called spring tides. When all these factors occur and the moon is positioned at its closest point to earth, its gravitational pull is the greatest, creating the very high tide of today.

Neap Tides

When the sun, moon and earth line up at right angles to each other, smaller water bulges create neap tides that occur about one week after spring tides.

Finally the young woman wrangles the squirming kids back into the stroller. Knowingly, the grandfather smiles at us and we all relax again.

An Earlier Journey

An earlier journey in springtime also brought us to Fletcher's Cove. Then we were not in the aftermath of a storm, but still under the influence of a

Fletcher Cove platform

full moon when advancing high spring tides washed out plans to walk our way south to Solana Beach starting north in Encinitas.

Located south of Carlsbad and north of Del Mar, Encinitas, constructed on beach and dune ridges, rises about

100 feet above the sea. Known as the Flower Capital of the World, it celebrates in November by massing Christmas poinsettias for holiday flower tours. In the spring and summer, the mesas of Cardiff-by-the-Sea, named for a seaport in Wales, explode with the colors of fuchsias, ranunculus, begonias and avocados.

Homes dangle atop bluffs where natural sea caves and tunnels, coupled with erosion from grading, contribute to the instability of some cliffs. Collapsed and rebuilt stairways to the beach show graphically what the orange signs warn of: "Active cliff failures!" Staircase beach access points and viewpoints are sandwiched between the bluff-top homes that have urbanized the cliffs.

Grandview Stairway, Encinitas (Leucadia)

At the Grandview stairway in residential Leucadia, we descend a newly constructed flight of steps ushered along by squat palm trees. The vista reveals itself with a punch! Without the blinders of the homes, it's as if a wide-angle lens has opened to include sweeping coastline and an ocean as blue as a marlin.

When English colonists settled and surveyed this part of the coast in 1885, they called it Leucadia, Greek for a "sheltering place."

The view may be wide but at high spring tide, the Grandview Beach narrows to a rocky strip. Still, today it meets the desires of a fisherman and several surfers willing to make the trek down the staircase.

Beacon's Beach, Encinitas

At Beacon's Beach a primitive trail snakes down from a view parking lot to three miles of narrow beach. Mom sits this one out, preferring to drive the picturesque residential streets above with Dad while I navigate the trail. I run, planning to end at our next challenge, Stone Steps stairway.

All of the sand is under water today leaving only slippery wet rocks to navigate. Close to getting caught by the advancing rollers, my feet beat the smooth polished stones making a sloosh, sloosh sound. Cliffs boom as breaking waves release their energy, bouncing the echo back out to sea. Few surfers brave the high tide. When rocky outcroppings preclude further advancement, I retrace my steps and mentally plan a new route on the city streets above. But when I arrive back at the bluff top, my partners had surmised a retreat and had returned to retrieve me.

Moonlight State Beach

In the early 1900's, locals favored the wider Moonlight State Beach down the coast for picnics held under the stars. Today workers apply a fresh coat of sand over the rocky sections of the beach, a spring ritual. Avocets are known to frequent these beaches.

D Street Stairway

Nearby, the D Street stairway, originally built in 1977 and damaged by storms in 1978, now has a new look and provides one more access down the formidable cliff. For those with no desire to drop off the edge to the bottom, there are the viewpoint day parks at H and I Streets.

Viewpoint Day Parks

At H Street, seated at a picnic table, Mom and I remark how the voracious tide has finally relinquished its claim to the sand. Mom hears the ghost voices of Cabrillo's sailors whispering in the forlorn wind off the ocean. I tell her they only stopped at a few places along the southern California coast, and probably didn't stop here anyway, too steep a climb! She gets tired of the wind pulling at her brown silk hat and takes her musing to the car.

Intertidal Zone

I focus on the intertidal zone far below. Like a mirror, the shallow water reflects the sun. Seagulls cry, swooping along the mirror to feast on the marine life. A lone hiker advances along the wet sand. The impressions of his footprints remain only a few moments then disappear as the seawater erases all traces. A family walks like sand crabs over the exposed tide pools.

Now worn out by the stair stepping and tide dodging, Swami's and the meditation gardens of the Self Realization Fellowship grounds promise a refuge.

Swami's Park

The Self-Realization Fellowship Hermitage dome now before us glints gold and white and looks as if it could have been transported from India. The original 1938 temple, built 30 feet from the cliff edge, collapsed in a landslide a few years later. Nearby, Swami's Park surprises us with sheltering old shade trees and picnic tables on the bluff. Stairs drop us down the face of an adobe-brown precipice to the prized surfing beach below.

Meditation Gardens

Back on the bluff-top, we proceed cautiously up to the Meditation gardens. We find terraced, shady gardens that soothe others and us with flowing fountains and flowerbeds. No one speaks. Only the ocean roars. A perfect end to our stair-stepping, tide chasing day.

~ Travel Notes ~

Solana, Cardiff-by-the-Sea, and Encinitas beaches are south of Carlsbad and north of Del Mar along Old Highway 101.

To reach Solana Beach, exit Lomas Santa Fe on Interstate 5 and proceed west. Fletcher Cove Park is at 111 S. Sierra Ave. and has picnic tables. Tide Beach Park is at Pacific Ave. at Solana Vista Dr.

To reach Encinitas, exit Interstate 5 at Encinitas Blvd.
Swami's is west of Old Highway 101 in Encinitas about 1 mile
south of Encinitas Blvd. Grills and picnic tables are in the
bluff-top park. Self-Realization Fellowship Hermitage Grounds
is adjacent up the coast at 215 K Street. The meditation
gardens are open to public.

Encinitas View Point Parks are at west ends of D, H and I
Streets off Old Highway 101 in Encinitas. They have picnic
tables and benches.

Moonlight Beach is at 4th Street at the west end of
B Street in Encinitas. It has picnic tables and fire rings.

Encinitas Beach is between Beacon's Beach and Stone
Steps Beach and has access only from Stone Steps or Beacon's
Beach.

Beacon's Beach is at the west end of Leucadia Boulevard
in Encinitas. The Grandview Stairway is at the west end of
Grandview Street in Encinitas.

Tandori Chicken Legs

8 chicken legs
8 tablespoons curry paste
1 cup plain yogurt
2 tablespoons lemon juice

Skin chicken legs and make three or four deep cuts to the
bone. Mix yogurt, lemon juice and curry paste to form
marinade. Coat chicken with half the marinade and insert
some into cuts. Let sit for 2 hours or overnight in the
refrigerator.

Preheat oven to 500°. Place chicken in a baking dish and
bake 15 minutes. Turn and spoon remaining marinade over
chicken. Bake another 10 minutes. Broil 5 minutes on each
side.

Pack for the beach in insulated container to serve warm.

Tabbouleh with Romaine Scoops

1½ cups of bulgur wheat
1½ cup each Italian and curly parsley
½ cup fresh mint
½ cup fresh cilantro
4 green onions, chopped with green tops
1 small clove garlic, minced
12 cherry tomatoes, halved
½ cup olive oil
½ cup lemon juice
Dash of hot sauce
Salt and pepper to taste.
One seeded red pepper cut into julienne strips
12 Kalamata olives
2 heads romaine lettuce, small inner leaves

Cover bulgur wheat with boiling water and allow to stand until grains are tender. (Approximately ½ to 1 hour.) Drain and pat dry with paper towels.

Wash, dry and chop parsley, mint and cilantro. Add green onions, chopped with green tops, garlic and cherry tomatoes halved.

Mix together olive oil, lemon juice, dash of hot sauce and salt and pepper to taste.

Combine all ingredients by lightly tossing with a fork. Cover the bowl and refrigerate several hours or overnight.

Cut one seeded red pepper into julienne strips and decorate top of salad with pepper and Kalamata olives. Serve surrounded with crisp inner leaves of romaine lettuce to be used as scoops.

Fresh Mango

Just before serving score skin of mango deeply from top to near bottom making four quartering cuts. Pull back skin from top revealing the flesh. Insert fork from bottom near center into mango. Serve on fork with plenty of napkins.

Trail of the Spa Waters

Visit downtown Carlsbad and drive beaches and the lagoon.

🍴

Angel Hair Pasta Aglio E Olio and Garlic Toast
Caesar in a Bag

Buena Vista and Batiquitos lagoons bathe the north and south ends of Carlsbad. A saltwater lagoon called Aqua Hedionda shimmers in the sun between them. But it is the mineral water from underground wells that christened this town, Carlsbad.

We start the TRAIL OF SPA WATERS at the corner of downtown Carlsbad at Main Street and Historic Highway 101. If it were the 1880's we would be standing in Frazier's Station.

Frazier's Station

The local newspapers touted it as a place where "Health, wealth and happiness are attained!" and thirsty passengers arrived by the trainload on the Arizona Eastern Railway. Mr. John Frazier offered them fresh cool water. They drank it with gusto with high hopes for its healing powers. Frazier had struck gold with the mineral water found when drilling his wells. Soon, into town marched another player, Gerhard Schutte. His dream was of a village of "small farms and gracious homes."

Gerhard Schutte

After buying Frazier out, he started a mineral water bottling operation and had the water analyzed. Amazing news arrived. The water's composition matched the therapeutic water much lauded in Karlsbad, Bohemia where Mozart,

Tolstoy and Beethoven came to "take the waters!" Seizing a marketing opportunity, savvy Gerhard reinvented the town as "Carlsbad."

Schutte Mansion

We survey Mr. Schutte's grand Queen Anne style mansion built in 1887. Our eyes run over rows of blue-gray wave-shaped shingles covering the exterior of the mansion, now Neimans restaurant. It is easy to imagine a demure Victorian lady peering out from the turret, impatient for news from a husband at sea.

Niemans Queen Anne-style mansion

Carlsbad Beaches

After lunch we take in the air and water, walking along the beaches. Plenty of oxygen from the flower fields is in the breeze. The hills of Carlsbad blossom every spring into a striped quilt of rows of thousands of red, pink, white and yellow ranunculus flowers.

Carlsbad City Beach

Bare-chested surfers, wetsuits hanging from slim waists, prop waxed surfboards against parked cars. Carlsbad City Beach, screened from view by homes and motels, has stairways leading to a slim, sandy strand.

Carlsbad and Robert C. Frazee State Beaches

Strollers along Carlsbad and Robert C. Frazee State Beaches navigate almost a milelong cement sea wall walkway. Many couples slide out of their coolers. Others stack firewood next to some of the few fire rings allowed on San Diego's North County
beaches. Kayakers and boogie boarders play in the tame surf. No one seems to mind the stack of the power plant dominating the skyline. Inland from this beach is Aqua Hedionda Lagoon.

Carlsbad sea wall walkway

Aqua Hedionda Lagoon

Pelicans, wimbrels and cormorants pick along the sedate lagoon water at Aqua Hedionda. I don't smell the odor of rotten eggs in the air today, but when Don Gaspar de Portola and Friar Juan Crespi's expedition forged the El Camino Real through here in 1769, they camped on the shores of this coastal lagoon near a Luiseno Indian fishing camp where something smelled to high heaven. Weary conquistadors and hungry missionaries probably with bad moods and blistered feet called this place Aqua Hedionda or "stinking water."

Most all of the southern California coastal wetland remaining is in the five lagoons and marshes between Oceanside and Del Mar. Batiquitos Lagoon on the east side of South Carlsbad State Beach is an important habitat for migrating birds.

South Carlsbad State Beach

Steps inside the campground lead down to a narrow beach covered with cobbles. These stones land on beaches from flooding rivers, sea cliff erosion and in this case possibly from dredging. Tides and seasonal storms also play a role.

Winter surf moved toward the coast by local storms breaks directly on the beach. The backwash carries the sand away, exposing pebbles and stones not usually seen in the summer. Summer swells break farther offshore in deeper water. Winter storms claim the sand. Summer swells should return it. But harbors, sea walls and dams have interrupted nature's balancing plan for the sand here. So sunseekers sit on stones. To escape the uneven footing, I bound up the cliff via a staircase to run past campsites with million-dollar ocean views ending our day in Carlsbad.

The word spa, derived from ancient French means, "taking the waters," going to a watering place or mineral spring. A few small spa hotels remain but "taking the waters" at the inland, exclusive La Costa Hotel and Spa is the main lure today. Frazier's well is no longer tapped but walking along Carlsbad seashores at sunset and swimming in the cool azurite ocean is like a day at the spa with only the cost of tired legs.

~ Travel Notes ~

To reach downtown Carlsbad from Interstate 5, take the Carlsbad Village Dr. /Elm exit. Turn right onto Carlsbad Village Dr. Turn right onto Carlsbad Blvd. The original well is at 2802 Carlsbad Blvd. in front of the Alt Karlsbad Hanse House.

Nieman's Restaurant is at 2978 Carlsbad Boulevard.

Carlsbad City Beach is accessed via a stairway west of Ocean St. between Pacific and Elm Avenues.

Carlsbad State Beach, (Tamarack State Beach) is west of Carlsbad Boulevard, between Pine and Tamarack Avenues.

The Aqua Hedionda Lagoon is east and west of Interstate 5 in Carlsbad.

South Carlsbad State Beach is 3 miles south of Carlsbad at 2680 Carlsbad Blvd. and Poinsettia Lane. The campground provides picnic tables, grills and fire rings. The Ponto day-use area, south of campground, has picnic tables and grills. Web site: www.parks.ca.gov

Angel Hair Pasta Aglio e Olio

This recipe is adapted from backpacking to the beach. Angel hair pasta cooks fast over a camp stove.
1 pound angel hair pasta
3 cloves garlic, finely minced
2 tablespoons olive oil
Red pepper flakes to taste
1 cup shredded Parmesan cheese
Salt and freshly ground pepper
Parsley, chopped

Pack all the ingredients including a pan for boiling the pasta, a small pan to sauté garlic, strainer, small cutting board, knife and a container of water for boiling pasta.

At the beach set up a camp stove and on low heat warm olive oil. Add minced garlic and sauté several minutes. Add red pepper flakes, salt and fresh ground pepper to taste. Sauté until golden brown, about 2 minutes. Set aside.

Boil the water for the pasta and cook al dente, (firm to the bite.) Drain pasta well. Toss with olive oil, red peppers and grated Parmesan cheese. Top with chopped parsley.

Serves 4.

Spa Caesar in a Bag

1 head romaine lettuce
Dressing
3 tablespoons olive oil
⅛ teaspoon dry mustard
⅛ teaspoon black pepper
¼ teaspoon paprika
¼ teaspoon salt
¼ cup grated fresh Parmesan cheese
1 clove garlic, minced
Juice of 1 lemon
½ teaspoon Worcestershire sauce
Anchovy paste or anchovy filets, as desired
Croutons

Place washed, dried and torn romaine lettuce in a large zip lock bag. Refrigerate.

Shake in mustard, pepper, salt and paprika and Parmesan cheese. Shake well. Refrigerate.

Whisk together all other ingredients and place in a shakable container.

To serve, shake dressing well and add with croutons to bag and shake. If desired, garnish with 2 washed and dried anchovy filets or add anchovy paste to taste to dressing.

Grilled Garlic Toast

1 loaf French or sourdough bread
½ cup butter
3 cloves garlic, minced

Chop 3 cloves garlic finely and mix with softened butter. Spread on bread and warm on grill for several minutes. Or wrap in tin foil and heat over grill.

Trail of El Camino Real

Walk the Six Trails of San Onofre State Beach South

ᚠ
Drizzled Tomatoes
Grilled Salmon over a Wood Fire
Scott's Roasted Corn
Baked Granny Smith Apples

On the TRAIL OF EL CAMINO REAL, I walk along the trail on the bluff that runs the length of the Park. About every one-half mile a trail drops down the ancient cliff to the beach below, creating the 6 Trails of San Onofre State Park South.

Mustard Plant

On both sides of the bluff trail, the tiny yellow flowers of the mustard plant cluster on slender, asparagus green stalks. Not knowing its place as non-native weed, this specimen of the genus *Brassica* strains straight up toward the sun. It is not the state flower but I will crown it queen of the El Camino Royal—a lacy yellow frame for and a perfect complement to the primary blue ocean.

Historic Highway

This weed may owe its origin to a seed flung from the hand of a Spanish foot soldier or a missionary. More than two centuries ago it is said, mustard seeds were dropped to mark the way for the return on the narrow Indian path, which was to become the King's Road, El Camino Real.

What dismay must have overwhelmed these intrepid adventurers, when returning from Monterey, they discovered the ocean wind had scattered the hardy seed and obscured the

113

pathway. Even so, this yellow goodwill ambassador of the coastal terraces must have cheered the soldier, as it does me. The mustard speaks of spring renewal, optimism and expanding possibilities of new life in Alta California.

Could this path be the same one used centuries ago? The exact route of this El Camino Real corridor is not known as the use of the routes of the Spanish changed over time. Eventually this historic footpath did connect all the Missions of California. Today, U.S. 101 closely follows this "King's Highway." Abandoned stretches of the old 101 Highway along the bluffs here serve as an asphalt campground at San Onofre.

Trail 1

I had expected this pristine beach near the northern boundary of San Diego County and close to San Clemente to be crowded with Spring Break visitors. Yet only a scattered few surfers walk down Trail 1 to San Onofre Beach below. These wild beaches at the end of steep and lengthy trails are still the secret of San Onofre.

My feet sink down into the deep wet sand of the sloping shoreline. Out in the ocean, cobblestones lurk and breaking waves bring them in to pummel tender anklebones. Above my head, cliffs like worn-down chimneys shoot up to an infinite sky. Then they collapse into deep brown canyons created by landslides.

San Onofre Nuclear Power Plant

The double-domed nuclear generating plant at the north end of the Park slices deeply into ancient San Mateo sandstone. This colossal concrete monument provides modern day energy.

Christianitos Fault

Intriguing earth history unfolds to me as I look up. Time is marked on the bluff walls. Four distinct wave-cut platforms, like bookmarks, display where the flat expanse of sea floor existed at different times. The Christianitos fault snakes along the cliff wall. Geologic studies date the age of the undisturbed wave-cut platform that carves through the fault to be 125,000 years old. Thus the fault is thought to be older and is considered officially inactive.

Trail 2 and Trail 3

I arrive at Trail 3 by walking south down the beach. Amid empty echoes in an empty Park, my heart and the surf pound as I scramble up Trail 3 on a single track through a green jungle of peppery chaparral.

View from Trail 3

Trail 4

At the top of Trail 4, I sit on a bench before dropping down its steep and loose dirt path. White scallops of breaking waves wash the curve of the coastline. People on the beach appear as specks on the sand. I take giant steps over logs laid out as a partial staircase through the Lemonadeberry and the feathery Coastal Sagebrush. Scrambling to hold my footing, I am delivered back down to the beach and walk on the wet sand past tower number 5. Soon I find myself at the infamous Trails Number 6 at the south end of the Park. This section of beach has attracted many more visitors.

Trail 6, Clothing Optional

Trail 6 has a reputation for being "clothing optional." State parks don't have nude beaches but it is tolerated unless there are complaints. The adjacent military-controlled beach means the clothing-free are probably watched with high-powered binoculars. I want to get a taste of the beaches beyond the Park border, so I decide to keep running.

The "au naturel" portion of beach must be farther down the coast. Everyone still wears shorts and T-shirts. Suddenly, two nude older men just a few feet ahead distract me—their portly bellies not a pretty sight. Whoa! That's my sign to go back. Doing an about face, I dash only to find all the beachgoers I had just passed have now stripped. I am the weirdo wearing long pants, T-shirt and big hat wielding a camera! I navigate along the shoreline past the naked bodies in my path. Head down, I charge like a bull away from the ocean looking for an escape.

The Canyon Escape

Spying a sunken canyon with a slot up the middle, I take my chances on the unknown rather than face the circle of twelve naturists before me. Fortunately, it is not a box canyon and delivers me up to the bluff at the southerly end of the Park.

Here, surfers at a campsite play conga drums. Their beat fills the air encouraging my flagging steps. I flash to another time when the Native Americans, loving music, played simple drums made of skins and hollow logs, maybe even here, to the accompaniment of flutes and rattles made of deer hooves and turtle shells. They probably were clothing optional, too.

Summer Solstice Return to Trail 5

On the day of the summer solstice, I return to the Park and shoot down the narrow slot canyon of Trail 5. Stunned, I stand on the wide beach next to the rumbling sea and marvel at the perspective from my viewpoint. The afternoon sunlight filters through wisps of clouds to highlight miles and miles of barren sea cliffs eroded into varied and fantastic forms like desert badlands. The illuminated faces of the sea cliffs are golden-white rilled San Mateo

Fantastic sea cliffs of Trail 5

sandstone. This is cut off abruptly by a horizontal wave-cut platform covered with a narrow marine boulder layer. A thick dark reddish-brown sedimentary deposit caps the top. New awareness and appreciation for this Park and these ancient cliffs comes from Trail 5 observations.

Egyptian Saint Onuphrius

The Park name, San Onofre, honors the Egyptian Saint Onuphrius. The sphinxes and pyramids of Egypt rise above the burnt sienna sand of the desert. The four marine terraces of San Onofre rise above an ancient shore. Never would you mistake San Onofre for Egypt but like Egypt, it is exotic, remote and powerful. This is a place where visitors can sleep along the King's Royal Highway, El Camino Real.

~ Travel Notes ~

San Onofre South State Park is 3 miles south of the city of San Clemente. From Interstate 5 exit Basilone Rd. and proceed 2.5 miles south along Old Highway 101 to the entrance.

The 6 Trails are marked on the bluff top and down on the beach, the numbers on the lifeguard towers correspond to the trail numbers. They are spaced about every one-half mile. Trails may close due to conditions.

The campground and day-use picnic areas have fire rings, grills and picnic tables. No facilities on the beach. Web site: www.parks.ca.gov

Grilled Salmon over a Wood Fire

John Klink, graduate of the Culinary Institute, New York and San Francisco chef, contributed this recipe.

Salmon, sea bass or any other local higher fat fish work best for this recipe. Leaner fish like ahi or shark will dry out.

2 pounds salmon
Lemon
Fresh dill
Sea salt and freshly
Ground pepper

Squeeze juice of 1 lemon over fish and place sprigs of dill on top. Start wood fire about 45 minutes before cooking. Burn down to a nice bed of coals and when flames have died down, place fish above the fire on a grill top or in wire basket coated with cooking spray. Cooking time will vary with beach conditions and heat of the fire. Cook about 5 minutes a side per inch of thickness. Turn fish once. Fish is done when flaky.

Remove to warmed platter garnished with fresh dill sprigs. Serve with hot mustard or horseradish sauces on the side.

Lemon halves wrapped in mesh or linen and tied with a ribbon are a nice touch.

Serves 4.

Grilled salmon over a wood fire

Hot Mustard Sauce

¼ cup dry mustard
¼ cup brown sugar
2-3 tablespoons warm tap water

Stir together mustard powder and sugar in a small bowl. Beat in warm water until thickened. Refrigerate.

Horseradish Sauce

½ cup mayonnaise
1 tablespoon chopped dill pickle
1 tablespoons horseradish or to taste

Stir together ingredients. Refrigerate an hour before serving.

Drizzled Tomatoes

Slice 4 vine ripened tomatoes and 1 red onion. On serving dish overlap tomato and onion slices. Drizzle with ½ cup mayonnaise whisked and carefully thinned with milk until pourable. Season with salt or pepper and dill to taste.
Serves 4.

Scott's Roasted Corn

Carefully pull back husks and remove silk from corn. Replace husks and wrap tightly in tin foil. Allow about 2 ears per person. Quarter limes. Pack a pepper mill, hot sauce, hot mitt and tongs.

At the beach, allow fire to develop coals. Place corn into coals. Roasting will take up to 30 minutes depending on the heat of the fire. Turn occasionally. Unwrap and squeeze limes over corn. Sprinkle on hot sauce and pepper.

Baked Granny Smith Apples

1 cup white sugar
1 teaspoon cinnamon
Granny Smith apples

Peel, core and halve apples allowing one per person. Combine sugar and cinnamon. Place apple halves on foil and sprinkle with mixture. Wrap and tightly seal edges.

Place the packets on outside of grill while main meal cooks. Cook 30 minutes or until centers of apples are soft. Serve in bowls.

Trail of the Surfer

Beach walk San Onofre State Beach North

𝅘𝅥

Volcanoes
Kratzers
Fruit Medley
Mimosas

Ask any amateur or professional surfer to name the high performance surf breaks at San Onofre. They'll tick off *Old Man's, the Point, Churches, Middles, Lowers* and *Uppers* of *Trestles Beach*. The Beach Boys glorified San Onofre with the 1970s hit *Surfing USA*. This beach reflects the personality of the surfers who claim it for their own.

The TRAIL OF THE SURFER includes a walk along cobble-strewn surf breaks. We arrive with the surfers streaming into the Park. When the ranger deems the lot below the bluff full, an orderly line forms on the cliff top. Then surfers are allowed in on a one-out, one-in, basis as latecomers replace the dawn patrol. We have never had to wait more than 45 minutes when the swells were up. Today we roll right in. Parked next to the beach on the sandy road are "woodies", trucks and motor homes.

Mediterranean Blue Door

Yesterday it rained. Today the usual milky blue haze is washed from the sky and it gives back the color of the ocean, which Mom calls the hue of a Mediterranean blue door. Brown, crenelated cliffs rise above us and completely isolate us from the outside world.

Whimsical Propellers

Handcrafted wooden signs designate surf breaks. Whimsical propellers spin atop old wooden longboards suspended on tall poles to tell of the sea breezes. Tenants of palm-thatched palapas hang up wet suits and prop surfboards against poles. Stands of tropical bamboo hide surfers rinsing off saltwater under the showers.

President Nixon

San Onofre is a 1971 legacy of President Richard Nixon. Five miles of formerly military controlled beach south of his Western White House was opened to the public. This preservation of 17 miles of coastal land adjoining Camp Pendleton maintains primitive beaches and keeps the watershed clean.

Longboarders at Old Man's

Longboarders like the well-formed, slower breaking waves here. This sport used to be for "old" surfers. But now young and old "hang ten".

Two sets of tandem riders give us a show. One hoists his girl partner and like gymnasts on a moving dance floor, they hold a pose while riding the wave.

There's love in the air! Love of the waves, love of the ocean, love of the beach and love between friends and family who have spent many happy hours together here. The long established San Onofre Surfing Club has been instrumental in the great care and welfare of this beloved beach.

Our Test Kitchen

Welcome to our test kitchen. In the glow of a beach fire at *Old Man's*, we tested many of the recipes in this book. That summer weekly taste tests were conducted at beach parties with friends and family. They laughed and we cringed at our flops, (tomato soup cake, plum consommé.) But they gobbled up our triumphs!

Our test kitchen

Dog Patch

There is one surf break I didn't mention, *Dog Patch*. Yup, just like it sounds, at the south end of the beach where the smallest waves break, a place where Daisy Mae, Lil' Abner and I might try surfing. Having to overcome an aversion to cold water and not being a good swimmer did not deter my desire to be a surfer. I enrolled in swimming lessons. I struggled. The day arrived when the swimming instructor loaned me his board and we had our last lesson here at *Dog Patch*.

Reality Check

The gray winter sky didn't calm the butterflies in my stomach. Neither did stepping into the 60° ocean water. I hoisted up the heavy longboard with difficulty. I paddled out what seemed like a mile to get outside the waves breaking in freezing cascades over my head and sloshing down the neck of my borrowed, oversized wet suit. Each time I caught a one or two-second ride on my knees, the heavy board surged like a battleship all the way to shore. I lost the swimming instructor in the glaring light.

I stood alone on this beach and faced reality. I was not cut out to be a surfer. I wanted to be cool but the cold ocean water made the cruel decision for me. Stick to boogie boarding on the white wash on hot summer days!

Surfers ride the energy of swells arriving here from

hundreds of miles away. They know what it's like to have the barb of a stingray in a foot, to have dolphins play on the waves with them and to have a board broken by a bad wipeout. They know the tides daily rise and fall. At "Sano," as the local surfers call it, there is no age limit on surfing. At the beach, playing on the sand, all of us are forever young and smiling.

Boogie boarding San Onofre

~ Travel Notes ~

From Interstate 5 north, exit Basilone Rd. (This exit is south of the City of San Clemente and north of Camp Pendleton exits) Go left at the stop sign. Proceed 1.5 miles along Old Highway 101 then turn right following the Surf Beach access signs. At the stop sign go straight. Enter beach through the pay-parking kiosk.

From Interstate 5 south, exit Basilone Rd. Go right at stop sign. Proceed 1.5 miles along Old Highway 101 then turn right following the Surf Beach access signs. At stop sign go straight. Enter beach through the pay parking kiosk.

If the surf is up there may be a line to get into the beach. It usually moves very fast. For RV owners, the road down and along the beach is bumpy and dusty. Fire rings are available and there are a few picnic tables near the volleyball courts at *Dogpatch*. Alcohol is allowed in non-glass containers.

San Mateo campground is .5 miles inland, nestled between fields of strawberries and rolling coastal hills.

Volcanoes

After tasting these pastries in Mexico City, Mom adapted a recipe to make the small erupting volcanoes.

1 packet yeast
3 tablespoons lukewarm water
¼ cup flour
2¾ cup flour
¼ teaspoon salt
⅓ cup sugar
¼ cup vegetable shortening
2 tablespoons butter
3 eggs

Topping paste:
½ cup flour
¼ cup sugar
¼ cup butter
1 egg

Soften yeast in water. Mix in ¼ cup flour and let rise until doubled.

Stir together 2¾ cups flour and ¼ teaspoon salt. Pour onto bread board making a mound. Form well in center. Place yeast mixture into well along with ⅓ cup sugar, ¼ cup shortening, 2 tablespoons butter and 3 eggs, lightly whisked. Mix together and knead 8 minutes until surface is smooth and slightly blistered. Allow dough to rise in a cloth-covered bowl in a warm place until double, about 2 hours. Form into 20 balls and place on baking sheet.

To form paste, mix only until smooth flour, sugar, butter and egg yolk. Top each ball with this paste, flattening it slightly. Brush with remaining slightly beaten egg white and sprinkle with sugar.

Kratzers

A camp stove and cast iron skillet are necessary to cook Kratzers, a cross between a crepe and a pancake.

6 eggs
1 cup flour
1 cup milk
Pinch of salt
10 strips bacon
Syrup

To make batter, beat eggs well. Add flour gradually. Stir in milk.

For each serving fry 1 slice diced bacon until almost crisp. Pour batter over bacon. Cook over medium heat until almost set on one side then flip and finish cooking.

For kids, batter can be drizzled into shapes such as bears, cats, etc. Serve with fresh berries, butter and syrup.

Serves 4-6.

Fruit Cup Medley

Mix together 1 small can mandarin oranges, 1 small can pineapple bits, red seedless grapes or green grapes, diced apples. Stir in apricot marmalade or sugar to taste.

Mimosas

Serve Champagne and orange juice in acrylic fluted glasses.

Trail of Mission Dam and Kwaay Paay Peak

Hike the Kwaay Trail in Mission Trails Regional Park and visit Historic Mission Dam

π

Pan Bagna

"Look inside the theatre! You won't believe the library!" T.M. has already checked out the stone lodge-like Mission Dam visitor center with its high wood-beamed ceilings. Sunlight streams in through windows with panoramic views of broad valleys, ancient marine terraces and rocky hills draped and dotted with coastal sage scrub.

On the way to the library we pass sculptures and a show of whimsical Impressionist art featuring *Bumbling Bee and Blue Dragonfly*. Wood smoke scents the library. I scan the collection of bird books and learn the birds we heard at the Mission Dam earlier today may have been Common Yellowthroat, Yellow-rumped Warbler or Bullock's Oriole.

I would like to curl up in a chair near the fireplace with a cup of tea. We had visited the historic Mission Dam and hiked to the top of Kwaay Paay Peak this morning and I am relaxed. But there is so much more to discover about the landscape and how the ways of the Kumeyaay (koo may yay) people influenced San Diego.

Earlier in the day we stood on the bank of the San Diego River and began the TRAIL OF MISSION DAM AND KWAAY PAAY PEAK in verdant riparian woodland. In the tall Western Sycamore trees songbirds warbled, hidden from our view by large star-shaped leaves.

"Perfect weather, sixty degrees." T.M. pulled his walking stick from the trunk and hiked out on the Old Mission Dam.

127

Historic Mission Dam

Designed by engineers trained in Mexico using two thousand year-old Roman aqueduct designs and supervised by Franciscan missionaries, it was built between 1813 and 1816 by Kumeyaay Indian laborers. The Dam and flume brought a reliable source of water to the Mission San Diego De Alcala. Granite boulders and mortar made of limestone and seashells were used to build one of the oldest water projects in the western United States.

Standing out on the Dam wall, T.M. spotted bass swimming in the dark, clear pool. Water ran over the rocks in soothing procession. A mallard drake paddled in circles. We turned our gaze to Kwaay Paay Peak rising above the Dam to the south. This was our next destination.

Kwaay Paay Trail

As we jumpstarted up the Trail, a rabbit hightailed it lickety-split out of our way. Perhaps his ancestors had been skinned by Indians to make warm blankets.

"This trail doesn't waste any time going up," T.M. said wiping his brow with a red handkerchief.

Coast Sage Scrub

Our feet kicked up the reddish-brown earth strewn with sharp-edged rocks. Rapidly we rose out of the cool lush riparian habitat of the historic Dam. We crossed an invisible threshold and moved up into hot, dry brushland.

This land of knee-high green bushes is home to birds, snakes, lizards, rabbits and coyotes. Aromatic Black Sage, White Sage, Laurel Sumac, Mission Mohave Yucca, Manzanita and hundreds of other low-growing drought-tolerant plants dominate the hills. Walking in sage scrub usually means it is hot and there is little shade to be found. These remarkable plants survive on small amounts of moisture. The Park insures future generations will be able to walk among these indigenous southern California plants, so important in the daily lives of the Kumeyaay.

The Kumeyaay

We fell silent listening to the cadence of our footsteps, hearts thumping from the short steep climb. The the cool wind seemed to carry the voices of ancient Kumeyaay who migrated from the Colorado River area to San Diego over two thousand years ago. At one time this Indian nation's territory included most of San Diego and Imperial Counties in California and 60 miles into Baja, Mexico.

The White Sage on the slopes made a good shampoo and masked a hunter's human smell from deer, quail, rabbits, antelope and mountain sheep. It also improved spirits and purified the home.

"Look, Our Lord's Candle," T.M. pointed to a *Yucca whipplei* with a single 10 foot stalk of white flowers. The Kumeyaay used this plant as food, roasting the young stalk in ashes.

Kwaay Paay Peak

Taking steep steps, we gained an altitude of 880 feet quickly. After about 45 minutes we arrived at the top of Kwaay Paay, hot and perspiring. A raven announced our

View from Kwaay Paay Peak of the Fortuna Peaks

emergence at the summit of 1,194 feet. The view spins 360° to the Park's four other peaks: North and South Fortuna Peaks, Pyles Peak and Cowles Mountain. Cowles Peak is the highest peak in the City of San Diego at 1,592 feet.

We picnicked on a pile of golden granite rocks. Our sandwiches tasted good as we sat facing the Fortuna Peaks and peered down at the Father Junipero Serra Trail and the Visitor Center in the distance. Toes jammed boots on the way down the Trail. We heard the screech of a bird of prey. We dared to hope—an eagle?

Visitor Center

A short drive from the Mission Dam brought us to the 5.5 million-dollar glass and stone Visitor Center. T.M. went inside to check it out, while outside I meandered past neat interactive displays that played the Least Bell's Vireo warbling song. This endangered bird lives in the most poetic places: willow thickets and rose briars. I also heard the cry of a California Gnatcatcher. Biologists think they mate for life and use a kitten-like cry to locate each other. And when I pushed the button and heard the screech of a Golden Eagle, I learned this rare bird with a six-foot wingspan, sacred to the Kumeyaay Indians, hunts in the daytime and nests along the Mission Gorge. We did hear an eagle on the trail.

Later in the afternoon, I find T.M. petting the Mission Trails Park resident cat also called Kwaay Paay. Seems this feisty gold, cream and mostly black feline often disappears causing the staff to panic lest someone has let her outside. Jean, the docent, says she sends out search parties but Kwaay Paay has many secret places to hide in the labyrinth of the Visitor Center.

We admire a basket on display. Jean fills us in on the story of this "honey pot" basket made from a yucca stalk.

"But what about the holes?"

"They filled them with tar. It is made by Raoul Sandoval, a Kumeyaay living in Baja, California near Ensenada."

After we purchase the honey pot and a book called *Indians of the Oaks*, Jean hands us a bundle of White Sage tied with red yarn, a customary parting gift in the Indian tradition.

Plant Identification Walk

I want Mom and Dad to see this very special destination. The day we arrive mist swirls around the five peaks making them nearly invisible. But Mom and Dad are duly impressed with the warm and cozy atmosphere and excellent exhibits of the Visitor Center. Outside, we ramble through the Mission Trails Plant Identification Walk starting on the quiet terrace. Then, "Here come the kids!" A busload of happy schoolboys and girls burst on the scene and run up and down the amphitheatre laughing and shouting.

Solstice Observatory

Something I hadn't noticed on other trips is that the Park has one of only two known solstice observatories in San Diego County. The Native American observatory consists of a circle of stones with a bisecting line pointing to the place where the sun comes up on the winter solstice, December 22.

Out at the Dam site, Mom sits down on the ground to snap a picture of me on the Dam wall. We continue past the Dam along part of the easy Oak Canyon Trail, which Mom calls user-friendly.

Historic Mission Dam

Dad says "Is there a Dam we are coming to or was that it back there?"

"That was it."

"I was expecting something more like the Hoover Dam."

Mom says, "Come on—think what they had to work with in 1813!"

We get back in the car laughing. I ask, "Along with Mission Bay and Balboa Park do you think this Park to be one of the three jewels in the San Diego park system?"

"Yes," they answer. "An interesting and unexpected treasure."

~ Travel Notes ~

Due to the Cedar Fire conditions may have changed. To reach Mission Trails Regional Park Visitor Center from Interstate 5, exit east on Highway 78. Continue to Highway 15 south. (From San Diego take Highway 15 north.) Proceed to 52 east exiting on Mast Blvd. in Santee. Turn left on Mast Blvd, go under the freeway and turn right on West Hills Parkway. Take West Hills Parkway to Mission Gorge Road and turn right. Proceed down Mission Gorge Road 2.4 miles to Father Junipero Serra Trail. From the Visitor Center there is a one-way road to the Old Mission Dam.

The 2.4-mile roundtrip Kwaay Paay Summit Trail is on Father Junipero Serra Trail just across from the entrance to Old Mission Dam parking lot. There is Trail access also near the Kumeyaay Campground adding 0.2 miles to trip. Turn left on Mast Blvd, go under freeway and turn right on West Hills Parkway. Take West Hills Parkway to Mission Gorge Road and turn right. Proceed down Mission Gorge Road 0.2 miles and turn right onto Father Junipero Serra Trail to the Old Mission Dam parking lot entrance 0.7 miles farther on the right. The Oak Canyon Trail is also accessible from the Old Mission Dam parking lot. No admission fees. Web site: www.mtrp.org

Picnic tables at Visitor Center and at Old Mission Dam.

Pan Baana

A 12-14 inch round bread scooped out serves as a plate for sandwich ingredients

Slice the bread loaf in half horizontally. Hollow out all but an inch or so of the bread. The two halves fit together to make the sandwich. Brush inside of bread with olive oil and garlic.

Layer choice of ingredients until bread is filled. Spoon several teaspoons of vinegar over mixture if desired. Replace top and press gently together. Wrap tightly in plastic wrap and refrigerate for several hours with a weighty object compressing sandwich. Cut in wedges to serve. Serves 4.

Suggestions for fillings are:

Tomatoes, red or green peppers, olives, cucumbers, onions or garlic

Drained peperoncinis or Chile peppers

Tuna, anchovy fillets or luncheon meats

Mozzarella, cheddar, feta or goat cheese

Italian parsley, lettuce, sprinkling of fresh basil or dried oregano

Trail of San Pasqual Battlefield Historic Park

*Visit San Pasqual Battlefield State Historic Park,
hike Museum Trail and Orfila Vineyard walk*

ㅠ
Toby's Tapenade

Destiny drives us past the San Pasqual Battlefield Museum
just as a young woman in a long shirt of denim trots
down the hillside to Highway 78 to hang out the "Museum
open" sign. The timing of past trips and the Museum's
weekend-only hours never coincided until today.

We march into the Museum seeking answers to questions
raised by earlier exploration along the Park's trails. Why did
American General Stephen Kearny's Dragoons and General
Andres Pico's Mexican
Californios clash in the San
Pasqual Valley? How was it
possible that both sides
claimed victory?

San Pasqual Historic
Park Hiking Trail

More than a year earlier
on the TRAIL OF SAN
PASQUAL VALLEY we had
discovered a two mile round
trip hiking trail threading
through 50 acres of
undisturbed granite foothills of

Battlefield Museum Trail

135

the Peninsular range. Here we began learning about an "almost forgotten" battle of the Mexican-American War. Not a pivotal conflict but still the bloodiest in California history.

We trotted up hilly terrain to view the battlefield area across the highway. The battle took place in a cold rain in December of 1846 during the first year of the Mexican-American War.

Traces of white wispy clouds were painted on the blazing blue sky on the day of our hike. Prolific briars of prickly pear cacti reached out spine-ridden green arms toward us on the Trail. On a wet cold dawn nearly 160 years ago many men lost their lives in this Valley. We stopped to read a plaque mounted on an enormous granite boulder:

> *The State of California Honors with this*
> *monument the American soldiers who under the*
> *leadership of Brig-Gen Stephen W. Kearny,*
> *Captain Abraham R. Johnston, Captain Benjamin*
> *D. Moore, Edward F. Beale, U.S.N. and Kit*
> *Carson, the Scout gave their lives in the battles of*
> *San Pasqual between the Americans and Mexicans*
> *December 6-10, 1846.*

We ascended to an elevation of 650 feet where we could see the backside of the Wild Animal Park. An easy drop down the chaparral-covered hill had us finishing the Trail at the Museum near the bronze statue.

Second Visit

On our second visit we had rolled up silently to the gate below the Museum in our new gas-electric hybrid car. The gas engine and the brakes recharge the battery so there is no need to plug it in. And best of all it gets 52 miles to the gallon. While we waited for the expected ten o'clock opening, T.M. studied his owner's manual with the theme from the western movie *The Magnificent Seven* blaring from the CD player.

Somewhere in the brush a gnatcatcher mewed a kitten-like call. I got out to take photographs. Ten o'clock came and went. No sign of activity. Scrutinizing the sign, we couldn't believe we had forgotten! *Open weekends only.*

Without missing a beat T.M. launched us west past an organic squash farm, eucalyptus and palm tree nurseries, corn and sod fields, a dairy farm, orange groves and old wooden farmhouses fenced by briars of prickly pear to the Orfila Vineyards. This small setback had afforded us the opportunity to explore more of the San Pasqual Valley's 11,000-acre Agricultural Preserve.

Orfila Winery

An open door welcomed us at the Orfila Winery where other early birds were arriving. Our tasting began as baskets of crusty French bread invited a sampling of olive oil, hot mustards, spicy peanut sauces and savory salad dressings.

Outside, our feet shuffled on soft earth in the symmetrical vineyard. We witnessed spring's revival in new buds and growth of shoots and green leaves. Mr. Orfila, formerly a diplomat and third generation Argentinean wine-maker, carries on the Valley tradition started by Franciscan

Orfila Winery grapevines

missionaries. They grew grapes in the Valley in the 1700s when Spain claimed the land.

Picnic tables under an arbor encourage a lingering lunch. We left with bottles of wine, olive oil and spicy champagne mustard.

Third Visit to San Pasqual Battlefield Park

Finally today the third visit is the charm. Inside the Museum T.M. pours over the informative museum map where red arrows show Dragoon and Californio movements. From the glass observation area we view the battlegrounds on private holdings across Highway 78.

General Stephen Watts Kearney

General Stephen Watts Kearney, ordered by President Polk to seize California, sent a patrol to covertly scout the number of Californios making camp in the Valley. With only few and far-between trees available for cover and the ubiquitous glochids-ridden prickly pear cactus as well as other dry, thorny, bushes snapping as we hiked through, stealth must have been nearly impossible. It is said the patrol party made such a ruckus scouting they were discovered by the Californios. This confirmed for Captain Andres Pico, who had recently arrived with 100 Californios, that American soldiers definitely had arrived in the Valley.

At dawn December 6, 1846 destiny led General Kearney's weary Dragoons along a mountain ridge. Ordered to "trot," the Captain leading the men mistakenly descended the hill in a "charge." The Californios fired a few shots then withdrew. Dragoons pursuing the retreating Mexican soldiers found themselves in a trap. Soldatos with fixed bayonets slashed and stabbed with eight-foot lances. The Americans fired their howitzer. Pico's men retreated.

Battle over; 22 American soldiers lay dead or fatally wounded. Nevertheless, the Americans claimed victory for holding the field of battle. They stayed and buried the dead. The Californios, by inflicting the most casualties, declared themselves victorious. Five miles to the west, the Californios and Americans would engage once again on Mule Hill and skirmish for five more days.

The helpful docent in the long skirt volunteers to start the ten-minute video on the Mexican-American War. Just

over a month after
the battle here,
peace came as the
fighting in California
ceased and the
treaty of Guadalupe
Hidalgo marked the
end of fighting in
Mexico in 1848.

MUSEUM *OPEN* TODAY

San Pasqual Battlefield
State Historic Park

If fate finds you
in the granite
foothills along Highway 78 and you see the girl in the long
skirt hang out the *Museum Open* sign, forget your other plans,
turn the car around and experience the San Pasqual
Battlefield Museum and hike the chaparral-covered hillsides
into history.

~ Travel Notes ~

To reach the San Pasqual Battlefield State Historic Park
take Interstate 15 north from San Diego. Exit Via Rancho
Parkway and turn east 0.9 of a mile. Go right on San Pasqual
Road for 3.4 miles then turn right on Highway 78 following
the signs to the Wild Animal Park and proceed 1 mile beyond
to the Battlefield Park on your left. Each year there is a
reenactment of the battle on the Sunday closest to December
6th. Web site: www.sanpasqual.org

The moderate 2-mile round-trip hiking trail climbs to an
elevation of 650 feet. There is also an easy loop nature trail
that starts near the bronze monument and climbs to an
altitude of 525 feet.

There are beautiful shaded picnic grounds near the
Museum.

To reach Orfila Vineyards take Interstate 15 to Via
Rancho Parkway. Turn right for 0.9 of a mile. Turn right on
San Pasqual Road and proceed for 1 mile. Orfila is at 13455
San Pasqual Road, on the right.

To reach Orfila from the Battlefield Park, turn right Highway 78. Go 0.5 miles, then go left on Old Milky Way Road and left again on San Pasqual Road. After 4.3 miles turn left at Orfila. Information: www.orfila.com

There is a self-guided walk through the vineyard and a lovely picnic area under grape arbors with mountain views.

Toby's Tapenade

Toby Taeger, graduate of the California Culinary Academy and award-winning chef contributed this delicious tapenade recipe.

1 cup Kalamata olives, pitted
1 cup green olives, pitted
2 tablespoons capers
4 cloves garlic
2-3 rinsed anchovies
Juice of ½ lemon
1 tablespoon black pepper
¼ cup powdered Parmesan cheese
4 sprigs fresh thyme
1 cup olive oil

Process all ingredients except olive oil until well incorporated but not liquefied. Drizzle in olive oil until oatmeal like consistency.

Serve with crackers or on crostini. Keeps refrigerated up to 3 months.

Trail of Mule Hill

Hike or Bike Mule Hill Trail/San Pasqual Valley Trail,
San Dieguito River Park

A
Fruit of the Valley Compote

Charge into Mexican-American War history along the newest Trail of the San Dieguito River Park. Discover the location of a long-gone San Diego pioneer town and stagecoach stop. Climb up to Raptor Ridge for a view of the San Pasqual Valley. Then indulge in some real relaxation, sweep down the rural back roads of the City of San Diego's Agricultural Preserve.

We embark on the TRAIL OF MULE HILL at the Sunset Drive Trailhead near Lake Hodges and head past the Sikes Adobe Farm House. The Mule Hill/San Pasqual Valley Trail is a new segment of the Coast to Crest Trail, which in the near future will link the salt marshes of Del Mar to the near 6,000-foot high pine forests of Volcan Mountain near Julian.

Mule Hill/San Pasqual Trail

An easy 1.25 miles down the wide Trail, T.M. and I halt to get a good look at a bump of a hill with rock outcrops. Newly installed interpretive stations bear maps and images of the continuing saga of the 1846 Mexican-American War battle that started five miles to the east and was engaged in here for five more days.

Gazing up at the unassuming Hill on this quiet morning, I try to visualize the fight that broke out when sailors, soldiers, and volunteers commanded by Brigadier General Stephen W. Kearney drove off attacking Mexican forces and took this Hill for high ground.

"It doesn't look very high to me."

T.M. explains that it drops off sharply on the other side. A Californio siege of four days from below the Hill prevented the American forces from escaping to San Diego. These descendants of Mexican and Spanish families, mostly vaqueros and ranchers turned soldier, defended their land with ardor wielding eight-foot lances with lethal skill.

Kit Carson

As the engagement dragged on, one soldier, Army Scout Kit Carson and an unknown Native American, slipped past three lines of the enemy's cordon losing their shoes in the process. Barefoot they walked all the way to San Diego to summon help.

Back on the Hill, Kearney came to a decision to fight and a sergeant was killed and buried there. Later, he was reburied with other San Pasqual casualties in one gravesite at Fort Rosecrans National Cemetery in Point Loma.

In San Diego, Kit Carson found help. Commodore Robert Stockton ordered 80 marines and 100 sailors to Mule Hill. With the strengthened American presence, the Mexican soldiers withdrew. By then, Kearney's men had been so lacking in food they were reduced to eating their mules. Thereafter the Hill was dubbed Mule Hill. With reinforcements, Kearny's men marched on to San Diego completing a

Site of town of Bernardo

2,000-mile march that started in Fort Leavenworth, Kansas.

Bernardo

Just a short distance down the road, I find T.M. standing next to a low stonewall pointing to an empty field. "A town called Bernardo with a store, a public school and a blacksmith used to be there!

"What happened to it?"

"Wiped out when the Lake Hodges Dam project brought water to the area in 1919," T.M. says speeding on ahead.

Stagecoach History

I linger to read the stagecoach history of this Trail. For a short time Bernardo served as a stage stop for coaches going from Ramona and Escondido to San Diego and from San Diego to Yuma. I could almost hear the whip of a Jehu driver and the pounding hooves of horses pulling the "mud wagon" down this road. A map shows that the Trail was used as part of an Overland route from 1820 through the 1850s. And it is the route Kearny's Army of the West marched along in 1846. Gold miners used the road from 1848-1851.

Mule Hill and Bernardo behind us, we meander along the Trail following the curve of the San Dieguito River sharing it with many bikers, hikers and equestrians. At mile three, the San Dieguito Crossing, the Trail takes a 90° bend to the north and the flat wide road becomes a singletrack trudge up two-thirds of a mile with an elevation gain of 300 feet to Raptor Ridge.

Raptor Ridge

After a picnic at this halfway viewpoint, we realize we don't have the energy to go another five miles out and then ten miles back. T.M. makes the supreme sacrifice to go back and get the car while I finish the Trail.

With rapture, I drop down Raptor Ridge heading east coasting high above the fields of the 11,000-acre San Diego Agricultural Preserve. Farming and the dairy business have been carried out here in the Valley for over a century.

Agricultural Preserve

My wheels spin past oak groves where crows caw-caw. The sky becomes milky blue as the sun chases off the gray overlay of morning clouds. The Trail is painted gold with dry grass and edged in the emerald green of the fields and the deep hyacinth blue of mountain horizons.

Ysabel Creek Road Staging Area

Raptor Ridge

The Trail now parallels Bandy Canyon Road and at the Ysabel Creek Road Staging Area at mile seven, I learn an astonishing fact: 40% of all avocados grown in the U.S. are from San Diego County! The Trail goes along behind a cut- flower farm. Other farm acreage grows turf grass, fruits and vegetables. The dairy cows are the mainstay of the San Pasqual Valley.

The final leg of the Trail skirts through an orange grove and out to the Bandy Canyon Staging Area just off Highway 78. I finish the ride from Raptor Ridge in just under one hour.

Scenic restfulness is found in wandering far off the beaten path through the countryside of farms and ranches. The visionary people who created this Trail have given future generations and us a historic perspective and a pastoral retreat.

San Pasqual Valley Agricultural Preserve

144

~ Travel Notes ~

From I-15 take the Via Rancho Parkway, go east briefly. Turn right at Sunset Drive and proceed to the parking lot. The Trail heads east from the parking lot past the Sikes Adobe Farm House. From the Sunset Trailhead, it is 1.25 miles to the Mule Hill Interpretive Stations, 3 miles to the San Dieguito Crossing, 5 miles to Raptor Ridge, 7 miles to the Ysabel Creek Road Staging Area and 10 miles to the Highway 78/Bandy Canyon Staging Area at the east end. Most of the Trail is level except for the 300 foot of elevation gained in two-thirds of a mile climb to Raptor Ridge and the reverse from the other side. Since this is a long Trail, it may be advisable to leave a shuttle vehicle at one end.

The Bandy Canyon Road staging area at the east end of the Trail is 4.5 miles past the Wild Animal Park on Highway 78. Cross the bridge and turn right on Bandy Canyon Road.

The Ysabel Creek staging area is .25 miles past the Wild Animal Park. Turn right on Ysabel Creek Road. The staging area is on the left just before Bandy Canyon Road.

San Dieguito River Park Information: www.sdrp.org

Fruit of the Valley Compote

8 cups of bite size pieces of:
Nectarines, Plums, Blueberries, Apples, peeled Grapes

2 tablespoons lemon juice
1½ cups water
¾ cups sugar
1 tablespoon fresh ginger, peeled and finely chopped
2 whole cloves
1 cup dry red wine

Place fruit in a plastic bowl. Toss with lemon juice. In saucepan, combine water, sugar, ginger and cloves. Bring to a boil and simmer 10 minutes. Add wine. Cook for one minute. Add fruit and simmer until fruit is tender but not mushy. Refrigerate. Serve in bowls with a spoon. Serves 6-8.

Trail of Clevenger Canyon

Hike the Clevenger Trail South, San Dieguito
River Valley Park, visit San Pasqual Store

A

Country Picnic Hero Sandwich with Dressing

Wind shivers through the rounded crowns of Coast Live Oak trees. The rustling of the shiny dark green leaves imitates running water but the ravine is dry. It is but a short easy hike to reach this cool riparian island within a sea of mixed chaparral. After climbing to a 1635-foot summit overlooking the San Pasqual Valley, we look forward to revisiting it on the way back down the Trail.

San Pasqual-Clevenger Canyon Trail South

The Clevenger Canyon Trail South trailhead is a few miles east of Bandy Canyon Road on Highway 78. T.M. and I lace up our new hiking boots, pull on hats and hit the TRAIL OF CLEVENGER CANYON ascending the south side of Santa Ysabel Creek Canyon.

This Trail is part of a vast trail system plan following the 55-mile corridor of the San Dieguito River, from the desert just east of Volcan Mountain near Julian to the San Dieguito Lagoon salt marsh in Del Mar at the Pacific Ocean. It is about midway on the watershed within the San Dieguito River Valley Park in the San Pasqual Valley.

Below us, slow-snaking Highway 78 is a river of semi-trucks downshifting on the steep Clevenger Grade. The deep green acres of farmland in the agricultural preserve contrast with the olive-gray chaparral of the steep surrounding hillsides. T.M. pulls out his new binoculars and focuses across the canyon spotting the longer and more difficult North

147

Clevenger Trail zigzagging up and over the ridge on the other side of the Valley.

He asks, "Who is Clevenger?"

"I don't know. We have to find out."

After .5 miles of easy hiking we arrive at a fork in the Trail. We could go east or we could go west, just like Bob Seger when he had to choose in his 1980s song *Roll Me Away*. Bob had a young hawk to show him the way. We check the map, look for a hawk and head east.

Coast Live Oak

After another .4 miles of walking, we drop down into a gulch shaded by Coast Live Oaks. These trees are the common oak found on the coast and the foothills of San Diego and I think have come to symbolize the good country life of Old California.

Poison oak lurks at knee level ready to ambush an unsuspecting trespasser. We step gingerly around this plant of the cashew family. To those sensitive, a slight brush against a leaf or stem may cause an itchy reaction to the toxin. Even though the temperature is a mild 64°, T.M. wipes his brow as we appreciate this island of coolness before crossing a wooden footbridge that delivers us out in the noonday sun into a patch of spicy Chamise, Black Sage and Lemonadeberry.

Coyote Highway

The footpath widens into an old jeep road. We both remark this Trail seems to be a coyote highway judging by the numerous scat piles and recent body imprints of sleeping coyotes on the low-lying bushes. The thick almost impenetrable underbrush makes good dens for these shy animals that eat mostly fruit, insects and rodents.

Eyes open for snakes, we see instead a Western Fence Lizard darting across the path. The color of their backs closely matches the hue of the granite outcrops. They have also

adapted to blend in with the color of burned Chamise, a
chaparral shrub found on southfacing slopes like these.

Much of Clevenger Canyon burned in 1993. One way
that Chamise regenerates after a fire is with the huge amount
of seeds the plant drops that can lie dormant in the soil for
centuries. Fire cracks open the dormant seeds aiding
germination.

Yucca Whipplei stalks shoot up to the blue sky. After one
blooming season, they die. The dry gray remains of old plants
are strewn along the trail. Scattered quartz veins make us
wonder if there are any gold veins in these hills.

The Batholith

A raven up in the sky circles above what looks like an
enormous round boulder. Up close it resembles the "world"
that Atlas, the great Titan
giant was tricked into eternally
shouldering as punishment for
fighting with Zeus, the sky god
of Greek mythology—but
these rugged hills are not
dotted with loose rocks. What
we see is the weathered face of
the upper margin of the
batholith, a large body of
intrusive igneous rock believed
to have crystallized below the
earth's surface. The sandy red
remains of the solid granitic
rock form the fertile soil of the
river valley.

*Weathered face of upper margin
of the batholith*

Viewpoint

A few yards from Atlas's world, an offshoot Trail climbs to
a viewpoint. We scramble through the Chamise and T.M. lends

me a hand and hauls me up to the top of the 1755-foot summit for a look-see.

Cuyamaca Peak lies to the southeast. Northeast, deep purple Palomar Mountain rises in the distance. Signs of civilization poke out on hilltops. Telephone poles string the hillsides. Hilltop estates protrude. The back roads of Ramona cut gashes through the chaparral. The cold wind hurries us down off the boulder to return to the main Trail, which joins with another jeep road.

The Summit

The Trail heads north along a ridge. T.M.'s left heel is killing him and he is glad that we have reached our destination, a lower summit of 1635 feet.

Migrating Birds

While boosting himself up onto the outcrop, he steps on a White Sage plant scenting our picnic area with a savory aroma. Bees buzz on the ubiquitous Deerweed. At first,

Trail to the lower summit

I focus on the annoying urban sounds: the beeping of a backing up truck, shots from a far off gun club and grinding chainsaws reverberating up the canyon. All this is forgotten when we spot two large white birds on a flight path between north and south Clevenger Canyon. Perhaps they are migrating Canadian Geese or White Pelicans in graceful flight down the corridor of the San Dieguito River to Lake Hodges or the San Dieguito Lagoon on the coast.

It is a rare sight but golden and bald eagles still occasionally soar above the Park. From our aerie view we scan the San Pasqual Valley, Clevenger and Boden canyons. From this distance, the slopes draped in chaparral look as if they are covered by a solid gray-green blanket but the variety and details of each plant can be appreciated from walking trails such as these. We retrace briefly the way we came through the woodsy haven. Within 2½ hours including side trips we are back at the Trailhead.

San Pasqual Store

A short distance west on Highway 78, the San Pasqual Store on the north side of the road intrigues us, advertising "hot rocks and cold beer." Inside we pick through the gems and minerals. The store has a bit of Hollywood history. Jack Haley, who played the Tin Man in *The Wizard of Oz*, owned the store and nearby ranch in the 1940s. I find a book for sale on the counter titled *The Spirit of San Pasqual* by Mary Keiser. Here we find our answer to the naming of the Clevenger Trail.

After the Mexican-American War the San Pasqual Valley Mexican ranchos fell to the Americans. In 1872, John Clevenger, his wife and five children settled in the San Pasqual Valley. Their ranch was located on the south side of Santa Ysabel Creek. The canyon and road bear their name. The ribbon of Highway 78 cuts through Clevenger Canyon to the town of Ramona along the Clevenger Canyon Grade.

With the aid of this book listing all the historic homes of the San Pasqual Valley, we learn the Clevenger home still stands on Bandy Canyon Road with the distinction of being the oldest home in the Valley.

Historic San Pasqual Store

Thanks to the San Dieguito River Valley Open Space Park, we can experience the land almost as the Clevenger family would have enjoyed the good country life of Old California.

~ Travel Notes ~

From 1-15 exit Via Rancho Parkway east. Turn right on San Pasqual Valley Road. Follow the signs to the Wild Animal Park. The southern Trailhead is 5.3 miles, and the northern trailhead is 5.8 miles east of the Wild Animal Park on Highway 78. The south trail is a moderately easy 4.4 miles out and back not including side trips. The north trail is more difficult and up to 20 miles roundtrip. San Dieguito River Park web site: www.sdrp.org

The San Pasqual Store is 3 miles east of the Wild Animal Park. *The Sprit of San Pasqual: A Guide to Scenic San Pasqual Valley* by Mary Keiser is a good guide to the local history and homes and can be purchased there.

Country Picnic Hero Sandwich with Dressing

1½ pounds sliced ham or turkey
2 medium cucumbers, peeled and thinly sliced
2 onions, sliced
2 tomatoes, sliced
1 red pepper, seeded and cut into strips
½ head romaine lettuce, torn into bite size pieces
Dressing
½ cup each olive oil and rice wine vinegar
½ teaspoon sugar
2 cloves garlic, finely minced
6 French rolls

Prepare vegetables. Combine olive oil and vinegar with sugar and garlic in a shakable container. Shake well and let stand at least 1 hour. Arrange ingredients buffet style for guests to assemble sandwiches. Serves 4-6.

Trail of Nate Harrison

Mountain Bike up the Nate Harrison Grade Road to Silvercrest
Picnic Area on Palomar Mountain

☕

Orange Ambrosia Fit for the Gods

S teve is the reason T.M. and I are on this attack up the southwestern flank of Palomar Mountain. We emerge from thick coastal fog at the junction of Interstate 15 and Highway 76. We drive 12.7 miles farther along pastoral Highway 76. Turning the car up the Nate Harrison Grade lined with citrus groves, we park on the side of the road.

On the TRAIL OF NATE HARRISON, we single-file and pedal steadily up. We had never met Steve but a biking buddy had met him at a party and they had set a date to do this ride. We were invited to tag along.

Steve was a no-show this morning and that should have been our first clue as to what was in store for us — 4100 vertical feet of climbing.

Pauma Valley

We rise out of the sizzling Pauma Valley. The climbing pays off immediately with views to the coast where the fog still shrouds the landforms. Mexico recedes in the deep distance. The hot not so benevolent sun beats down on the neat rows of cultivated citrus trees on the hillsides. Motorcycles shifting gears whine shrilly racing along the roads below us.

At mile five, I find red-faced T.M. sitting dejectedly on the side of the road under a California Black Oak munching his sandwich—bonking big time. After food, rest and some mutual encouragement, we mount our bikes and resume climbing.

Ranch hands in old trucks drive past waving, flashing sympathetic smiles. Stiff-kneed and saddle sore, we push on and on and on.

Finally, after several hours, we reach an altitude where Jeffery Pines and Douglas Fir

Nate Harrison Grade Road up Palomar Mountain

trees cast deep shadows over the road. The shady lane renews our spirits for a brief moment before bugs swarm us as if we are cattle. Plagued by gnats, we steer with one hand and flutter bandannas to keep them at bay. We ride. We walk. We ride some more. Still the endless climbing does not stop. A small voice in my head urges me to call it quits. My head pounds. We ride on. After all if Steve had done it, why couldn't we?

We urge each other on until finally a sign on the road reads, "Palomar State Park headquarters 1.7 miles." Forty-one hundred feet of vertical conquered, for the first time in over three hours I am able to shift out of granny gear.
Flat, smooth pavement never felt so good!

T.M. mutters, "Thank heaven for small favors!"

Silvercrest Picnic Area

At the Silvercrest Picnic area at 5,000 feet it seems the trees welcome our arrival. The gnats are gone and we sit in a picnic area surrounded by old, enormous thick-trunked trees. Their fragrant scent revives us. After resting and refilling our water packs with fresh cold water, we button down for the chilly downhill ride.

Usually freefalling downhill is a great joy but after this punishing climb, each rut jars stiff necks, bumps tax tired legs and speed blurs the vision.

Finishing the 10-mile ride in 4 1/2 hours including our time at the top, T.M. remarks with sarcasm, "The only smart one today was Steve!"

But as with all difficult rides we soon forgot the pain in the real glow of accomplishment. Steve was the catalyst that pushed us beyond our limits to reach a pinnacle called Palomar. Thank you, Steve, whoever you are!

~ Travel Notes ~

From the Intersection of Interstate 15 and State Highway 76, proceed approximately 12.7 miles east and turn left on the Nate Harrison Grade Road. About 3 miles up, park off the road. Stay off private property and citrus groves. It is 18 miles out and back. Bring plenty of water. Additional water is available from a spigot in the Silvercrest Picnic area near Park headquarters.

Orange Ambrosia Fit for the Gods

The orange tree traveled from Spain to Mexico then found its way to California.

4 large navel oranges
6 tablespoons powdered sugar
1 cup coconut, flaked
3 tablespoons orange juice

Peel oranges and remove all outer white membrane. Cut oranges crosswise and cut slices into quarters.

Toss all ingredients together. Refrigerate one hour.

Serves 6.

Trail of Palomar Mountain

*Visit Palomar Observatory, drive to Boucher Hill Lookout,
hike the Doane Valley Nature Trail and Weir Trail to
Lower Doane Valley to Upper French Creek Trail*

ᚵ

Italian Focaccia Bread Sandwich

I solated and remote, the Palomar Mountain Observatory
houses William Ellery Hale's 200-inch telescope.
Competition is fierce for the very limited time available.

We start the TRAIL OF PALOMAR MOUNTAIN,
driving pastoral Highway 76 past horse farms, ranchettes and
roadside stands selling locally produced fruits and vegetables.
We whiz by hothouse nurseries and prickly pear-fenced old
farm homes, a welcome relief from urban sprawl.

Dad says, "I can't believe we drove all the way out here
from Minnesota in 1957, with three kids in the backseat of the
56 Ford on blacktop two-lane roads."

More than 40 years later, today we zig and zag up
mountain road S-6, the top of the mountain a mystery hidden
under a bank of white clouds. Mom points out granite
outcroppings of golden rocks, green hillsides strewn with
gigantic boulders and golden-yellow native California Poppies
blooming, with all four petals open to the sun, on the roadside.

"How did we end up at remote Palomar back then?" I ask.

"Dad did the driving, I controlled our itinerary to make
sure we explored everything from San Diego to San Francisco!"

Palomar Mountain is part of the Aqua Tibia Mountains of
San Diego County. We pass through the small town of Pala
with a new big time casino on the San Luis Rey River. Large
specimens of blue, pink and green tourmaline crystals have
been mined in this area as well as topaz and garnet gems. No
one knows why these rare minerals occur here.

157

Getting closer to our destination, Dad remembers that on the first trip we were able to gaze through the eyepiece of the telescope, I didn't remember anything about our trip to the Hale Observatory in '57; I was only six years old.

Now above the clouds, 5500 feet of altitude conquered, the sky is celestial blue. Stretching cramped legs, we walk out into the pine-scented dry mountain air along a path lined with needle-draped firs—perfect Christmas trees. Loud, happy cheeping emanates from the Gus Weber Picnic Grove but not mountain songbirds. Four busloads of freed fifth graders on cloud nine climb trees and picnic.

High noon. The imposing white 1000-ton rotating Observatory dome bathed in full sun shimmers like a moon in the sky. We

Mount Palomar Observatory

imagine the nighttime when the Dome opens and rotates for the study of stars, comets, quasars and asteroids.

George Ellery Hale

Inside the building rotunda, George Ellery Hale solemnly greets us—that is the bronze bust of the revered astronomer. One of his many discoveries was the magnetic nature of sunspots. His 100-inch telescope had been successfully installed on Mount Wilson Observatory in Los Angeles. By the 1920's, Hale and his fellow astronomers realized a larger telescope would be essential if research was to progress in the understanding of the universe.

Palomar Observatory

Palomar Mountain was selected as the site for this project in 1934. Corning Glass cast a 200-inch Pyrex glass disk and cooled it for eight months. The disk, then weighing 20-tons, had to be ground and polished. Delayed by World War II, the finished telescope mirror made the long-haul trip up the mountain road to be mounted in the telescope. Caltech astronomers began studying the light from celestial objects at Palomar in 1948.

The Observation Deck

Walking up 50 steps we enter the glass-walled deck. No looking through the eyepiece this trip! This is now strictly a working facility owned by the California Institute of Technology. Devices like infrared cameras and digital electronic detectors replace the naked eye. We are surprised to learn that astronomers can spend only a few nights a year using the telescope. Requests for time run 50% higher than availability. But that's not bad compared to the 1000% higher requests than availability of the Hubble space telescope orbiting above the atmosphere of the earth. Even at this elevation of 5,500 feet, city lights pollute the night sky obscuring the view. High pressure sodium city lights are named as the major contributor to "sky glow."

Exiting the Dome, we stop to admire a manzanita bush in full pink bloom abuzz with pollinating bees. A flash of dark gray and a cooing in the bush catches our attention. "A pigeon, it's a pigeon!"

Dad laughs watching us peer into the red branches to get a picture. "As if you haven't ever seen a pigeon before."

Mom pipes up, "No—It's a Band-tailed Pigeon. This Mountain is named for that bird."

Band-tailed Pigeon

Palomar means "pigeon haven" in the La Jollan Indian dialect and in Spanish means "pigeon house." Dad smirks still thinking of the ubiquitous urban bird that feeds on seeds and crumbs. The Band-tailed eats nuts, acorns and berries. The light gray stripe at the end of the tail makes the band.

Palomar Mountain-Boucher Hill Lookout

To enter Palomar State Park we drive back out S-6 and turn up S-7 and enter into clouds festooning the forest along the one-way loop to the Boucher Lookout observation point. The Boucher Hill firewatch tower erected in the 1940s for visual observation of wildfires stayed open seasonally until the early 1980s. Smog, haze and fog made it difficult to spot smoke and like the Palomar telescope, technology replaced the human eye for detection.

Now all the lightning ground strikes in the western states are recorded by satellite. Fire agencies investigate strikes for trouble using infrared photographs taken from planes.

Wisps of white clouds drift over the mountain obscuring the panoramic view over the Pauma Valley. The picnic area looks desolate in the cloud cover and the temperature is 49.° Chilled from the moisture, we head northeast toward sunny Doane Valley.

The Boucher Lookout Loop intersects the Nate Harrison Grade Road. I point out the dirt road T.M. and I had struggled up on mountain bikes swatting gnats to reach the top of the mountain from the Pauma Valley in 90° heat.

Doane Valley

We park at the Trailhead for the Doane Valley Nature Trail. A Stellar Jay looking for picnic scraps perches next to the sign listing just some of the eighty birds of the forest: Raven, Mountain Quail and Chickadee, White Breasted Nuthatch, Dark eyed Junco, Band-tailed Pigeon and the

Stellar Jay, the greeter himself, with prominent crest shrieking *shaack shaack shaack*.

Getting out of the car, Mom and Dad head toward the Doane Pond and it streams. I mention to them that the Trail starts right back here by car. I plan to take them on the easy .75 mile Doane Valley Nature Trail.

The Doane Pond

Waiting for their return, I unsuccessfully attempt to photograph bluebirds. Ten minutes go by but they don't return to the car. Anxious to start up the Trail, I head out to Doane Pond muttering, "Where are they?" Finally I spot them on the far side of the Pond.

I yell across the Pond, "Where are you going?" Mom points to the trailhead sign pointing to Scott's Cabin and Thunder Spring Trail. I wave them back to the parking lot.

"You never told us the Doane Nature Trail started here. How were we supposed to know?"

Dad says, "We were just going to go around the Pond anyway." The little Pond surrounded by cattails and stocked with trout is a scenic respite with nice level footing for them. But I have an agenda.

I drag them back to the parking lot. Mom starts up the Trail holding her purse over her shoulder. I insist she leave it in the car but she resists. Finally, Dad stows it in the trunk. "You won't need it."

Bunchgrass Meadow

Doane Valley Nature Trail

We pick up our Nature Trail guide with 30 points of interest and begin the narrow path. Wearing street shoes Mom has trouble right away. "I hate tennis shoes." She hangs onto Dad's arm, "We'll probably both go down," she laughs.

I have forgotten to bring extra water and hiking sticks for stability. After stop number 3 at Doane Creek we turn left and the going gets steep and muddy. Ten minutes later Dad says, "I'm going back." And they do.

I then realize the Trail arrow we followed was for hikers coming from the other end of the loop. I head the right way now but they are out of earshot. I sprint up the Trail and find answers to many questions we had asked about the plants and trees of Palomar.

White Fir and Incense Cedar Trees

How do you identify White Fir trees? Look for the light-colored bark. Incense Cedar, sometimes mistaken for a redwood tree, has similar deeply crevassed bark but has distinctive fernlike fronds of foliage, "scaly leaves that overlap the twigs."

I pass Berry Alley where favorites of the wild life grow: wild currants, raspberries and strawberries. Out in the sunny meadow I stop at number 16, a California Black Oak. It takes the large acorns two years to develop fully and the Band-tailed Pigeons consume large amounts of them. I'll have to tell Dad that one.

Canyon Live Oak and Ponderosa Pine

I learn why I have trouble identifying the common oaks of southern California. The Canyon Live Oak, coveted for its strength and sought after by pioneers, has evergreen leaves but they vary in size, shape and color depending on the age of the leaves. Most leaf edges are spiny but some appear smooth.

Lying next to a patch of wild strawberries, I shiver with my camera straight up the trunk of a Ponderosa that soars up into the blue sky. The Ponderosa Pine is visually similar to the Jeffrey Pine. But get up close and smell the bark. The Ponderosa smells like resin, the Jeffrey like vanilla bean.

A speed walk through the meadow, with one stop to touch the edges of the Deer Grass used by the Indians in coiled baskets, brings me to the campground and the Doane Pond parking lot.

Mom already knows about the trees I saw. Seems she sat on a split rail fence worried about me being alone in the forest and took the tour by reading the pamphlet guide. She identifies the noisy Stellar Jay that greeted us earlier and the California Lilac and Bracken Fern we had seen near the Palomar Observatory.

We wind our way back down Palomar Mountain out of the sunshine into the clouds and down S-6 to pastoral Highway 76. I recalled that information had been posted at the Observatory for those with aspirations to become an astronomer. Did any of the kids on the field trip now want to explore the age of the universe, the origin of the sun and planets? Where they amazed that light detected at Palomar from a quasar took billions of years to reach Earth?

Later that week, I heard an astrophysicist announce a planetary conjunction alignment. He said this naked celestial event could be observed without a telescope even in the sky glow of Manhattan in New York City. Two hours after sunset, I dragged T.M. outside. The sky clear of the usual coastal low clouds, we witnessed the alignment of the Moon, Venus, Mars, Saturn and Jupiter.

I don't know about the kid's imagination but after the visit to the Mountain named for a pigeon, I'm looking up at the night sky more often.

Postscript: Weir, Lower Doane Valley and French Valley Trail

In mid June, T.M. and I return to Palomar to hike the Weir and French Valley Trails. Escorted on the side of the Trail by white blooming azaleas and bright green Bracken Ferns, we reach the historic Weir site and climb up into the stone gauging station built around 1903 to assess the potential for generating electricity in Lower Doane Valley. But the possible dam site plans came to a halt when in 1933 the state purchased most of Doane Valley and it remained undeveloped state park land.

"I knew it! " T.M. peers into the dark creek water. "There are little fish in the pool. I think my dad and I hiked this Trail 35 years ago when I was 12 years old! Back then, the Creek supposedly had wild trout attracting fly fishermen."

T.M.'s father passed away several years ago and as we moved on from the Weir site, I silently wondered if T.M. remembered today was Father's Day.

We transitioned to the Lower Doane Trail from the Weir Trail and the forest opened up into golden bunchgrass meadows. Protected from grazing and overuse the meadows are returning to their natural condition, a highlight of the Trail. A hiker coming along the Trail through the grassland tantalizes us with news that we are in for another surprise up on the French Valley Trail.

The breeze keeps away the annoying gnats and ruffles the leaves of the dogwoods as we picnic on the bank of the now dry French Creek. Other hikers stop to inform us they just saw a rattler and last night a mountain lion!

Canyon Live Oak tree

Now on the last leg of the Trail, back under the cool
mantle of forest leaves, an unknown bird calls sweetly a seven-
note tune. I hear T.M. up ahead of me whistle back. And I
hear the bird answer.

Then T.M. calls out to me, "These are the biggest oak
trees I have ever seen!"

I catch up to him. The enormous gray trunk and
horizontal branches of a Canyon Live Oak tree dwarf him.

The oak trees seeming to grow right out of the boulders
are the largest of the western oaks. The twisted, gnarled trunk
trees differ from Coast Live Oak in that they grow at higher
elevations and are usually found in canyons. We guess this one
to be the one known as the Joaquin Murietta tree.

Back at Doane Pond two hours after we started, a young
boy and his father race past us with fishing poles. Now many
families ring the shore of the little Pond. They too will have
fond memories of being a kid on Palomar Mountain.

~ Travel Notes ~

From the intersection of Interstate 15 and State Highway
76 head east on Highway 76 for 20.5 miles. Take the Country
Road S-6 exit on the left. Follow to Palomar summit parking
lot at the Observatory. The Observatory is 8 miles east of
Palomar State Park and open to the public from 9:00 a.m. to
4:00 p.m. Admission fee: none

To get to Palomar State Park follow the directions above
but at the junction of S-6 and S-7, go left on S-7 following the
State Park signs to the end of the road. Park day use hours are
from 8:00 a.m. to sunset. Admission fees: $2 per car.

To reach the Boucher Hill Lookout by car from the Park
Headquarters, head west following the one-way loop road to
the end.

At the junction with the Nate Harrison Grade Road and
Boucher Hill Lookout Road, head north following the signs to
Doane Valley near the school camp. Doane Valley Nature
Trail starts in the parking area near the Doane Valley Pond.

There are self-guiding brochures in a box at the Trailhead. When the Trail ends inside the Campground, turn right and walk down past the Campfire Center to the parking lot where you began.

The Weir Trail also starts at the Doane Pond parking area. From the Doane Pond Parking area to the Weir is 1.2 miles. It is .7 miles from the Weir historic site to the Upper French Valley Trail. It is 1.3 miles from the Upper French Valley to Doane Valley Campground, making a loop trail of 3.2 miles total. All of these trails are easy with little elevation gain or loss.

It may be cool and cloudy on the Mountain. Bring layers of clothing and water. Web site: www.palomar.statepark.org

Picnic tables and grills are at Boucher Hill Lookout, Doane Pond and Silvercrest picnic area. If one side of the Mountain is cloudy, foggy and cold, try the opposite side where the sky may be clear and the sun shining.

Italian Focaccia Bread Sandwich

Cut sandwich size pieces from a large focaccia bread and split horizontally. Brush inside lightly with olive oil. Layer pepperoni, mozzarella, arugula, fresh basil, tomatoes, green or black olives, peperoncinis and sliced red onion. Wrap in saran wrap. Can be made a few hours in advance and refrigerated.

Trail of Gold

*Visit to Julian, tour of Eagle/High Peak Mines, walk around
Stonewall Mine/Cuyamaca City, mountain bike the Grand Loop
Trail in Cuyamaca Rancho State Park*

⚘

Grand Loop Trail Mix

T he mine foreman snuffs out a candle plunging us into
utter darkness. In the black silence, the Julian gold mine
comes alive and we become miners inhaling mouthfuls of dust.
Our stooped backs ache and ears ring from the rhythmic *pick
pick pick* of our axes striking solid stone walls. We follow the
quartz veins, the only place gold will be found. We ride up and
down eleven levels of tunnels in an ore bucket. We work in
dim light cast by a burning candle on a hat. Twelve hours of
hard rock mining over, we emerge from underground blinded
by the sun and gulp the first breath of sweet Julian mountain air.

On the TRAIL OF GOLD we begin in Julian, just 50
miles northeast of downtown San Diego. Julian was once a
gold mining camp. Today its attraction is being at the right
elevation, 4,500 feet, to grow apples. Local bakeries make
them into luscious pies for weekend visitors.

After a quick stroll along the false front store facades to
purchase an apple crumb, we tour the Eagle and High Peak
Mine.

Eagle/High Peak Mine Tour

Just a quarter mile up the main street of town, on Gold
Hill, we experience the gold rush days of Julian in the 1870s
starting at the Eagle Mine.

Twelve of us shuffle along the old ore cart track. Our tour
conductor—I call him the mine foreman—is no rookie; he

grew up here, knows the facts, details and history of Julian mining from placer to hard rock to modern mining techniques.

The Quartz Vein

The first fact of hard rock mining he drills into us is: "To find gold, first find the quartz."

Quartz? Aren't we searching for gold?

He huffs, "Gold" is found here only in quartz veins in the Julian schist."

We traipse behind him following the vein down dusty tunnels now lit by electric lights. Five tunnel levels run above us and five drift below. We are his "flat-lander" miners in the bowels of the mountain for forty minutes.

He invites us up fifteen steps to another level. Sitting at the foreman's desk, he lights a small candle and turns off the electric lights. We gasp in unison at the profound darkness of the underworld and fantasize the life of an underground miner.

We emerge from the High Peak Mine (the Eagle mining claim joins the High Peak claim in the middle) sniffing the good clean air, eyes squinting to adjust to the bright sunshine. The foreman talks as he walks us down through the pines and manzanita to the milling area. But my brain is saturated with mine facts and I hear only the wind and the cawing crows. Tragedy shut down the mines in 1907, when a superintendent and miner were killed in an accident. It is estimated the Eagle and the High Peak mines each produced between $25,000-$50,000 worth of gold.

Gold panning on the Eagle/High Peak Mine Tour

Trying our hand at placer mining, we pan for gold. I get ᵐᵘⁿⁱᵗⁱᵒⁿᵈ, I.M, ᵗᵃᵏᵉˢ ᵃ ʳⁱᵛᵉʳ ᵃⁿᵈ ᵃᶠᵗᵉʳ ᵃ ᵇⁱᵗ ᵒᶠ ᵈᵘˢᵗⁱⁿᵍ ᵃⁿᵈ shaking a few flakes of gold are revealed. We leave thanking ᵗʰᵉ ᶠᵒʳᵉᵐᵃⁿ ᶠᵒʳ ᵗʰᵉ ᵖʳᵒᶠᵉˢˢⁱᵒⁿᵃˡ ᵗᵒᵘʳ ʷⁱᵗʰ ᵃ ⁿᵉʷ ᵖᵉʳˢᵖᵉᶜᵗⁱᵛᵉ ᵃˢ to why gold is so expensive and understand the backbreaking ˡᵃᵇᵒʳ ᵒᶠ ᵃ ʰᵃʳᵈ ʳᵒᶜᵏ ᵐⁱⁿᵉʳ.

Cuyamaca Rancho State Park

In the fall when the sidewalks of Julian are six deep with meandering, pie-eating crowds it is good to escape to Cuyamaca Rancho State Park. Here miles of uncrowded biking and hiking trails wind through rolling oak woodlands and pine forests. The name comes from the Kumeyaay Indians, *Ah-ha-Kwe-ah-mac* "place where it rains," or *Kwee-muck* "the cloud lies behind the mountain."

Grand Loop Trail

In Cuyamaca Rancho, south of Julian on Highway 79, we park at the trout pond near the Boy Scout Camp and mount bikes to ride the 15-mile Grand Loop Trail. The afternoon Santa Ana wind blows hot and dry. We spin up the paved road. Before going onto the singletrack trail on the other side of a fence, we detour left a short distance to the Stonewall Mine.

Stonewall Mine

A harsh call from the Jeffery pines reminds that Cuyamaca City is "*Nevermore*," as quoted by the raven in the Edgar Allan Poe poem. The mine shaft sinks 630 feet into the ground and is surrounded by forest. It was abandoned in 1893.

In its heyday, Cuyamaca City piped in water, brought in telephone lines and built a hotel and even a library. The Stonewall Jackson mine, named for Confederate General Stonewall Jackson, got its name shortened to "the Stonewall" so as not to offend investors with Union sympathies. The richest mine strike in southern California, the Stonewall produced two million dollars worth of gold.

Back on bikes, we roll along the dry woodland meadow dotted with slow-growing, long-lived California Black Oaks. Their broad rounded crowns provide us shade. They provided the Kumeyaay with a favored crop, acorns.

Dry grasses flow over the graceful curves of the hills like spilled golden-yellow paint. A blueberry-purple suffuses the nearby mountains. After a moderate, steady climb, the descent is a steep fun-filled rock-strewn drop. At the bottom we collect our thoughts on the cool oak-shaded lane where the wind whispers in the crackling leaves of the stout spreading branches. The trail now follows the Sweetwater River.

T.M. ready to descend the Soapstone Grade

Green Valley

As we fly down Upper Green Valley Road, I half-expect to see a horse-drawn carriage trotting along the bowered road. In fact, the San Antonio stage line did run through the Park, then called Green Valley, on its way to the coast.

After riding eight easy miles in 80 minutes we lunch at a picnic table under the oaks at Park headquarters.

Cuyamaca Rancho Museum

Inside the Park Museum, we learn the Cuyamaca haven exists because in 1933 the generous Dyar family sold their Green Valley estate to the state of California for one-half of its appraised value. The stone house we are in was once their family home.

Prior to their ownership, James Lassator had bought the land from the Indians in 1855 and lived peaceably near them. The Julian gold rush of the 1860s brought hundreds of prospectors to the region eventually forcing the Kumeyaay Indians onto a reservation.

Back outside, a raven perched high in the oak tree reproaches us with a "gronk—gronk". Time to get back on the bikes to move on out the smooth road along Highway 79 for a brief section.

Japacha Fire Road

Turning west up Japacha fire road, the earnest climbing begins. Heads, necks and backs strain forward—up and up.

I swat at gnats swarming around my sweaty head. At Fern Flat fire road I halt for a rest, pop a Medjool date in my mouth and inhale the pungent scent of pine needles. Rejuvenated I pedal up through the White Fir, Incense Cedar and Ponderosa and Jeffrey pine forest.

Azalea Spring Fire Road

On the Azalea Spring fire road the uphill ascent is finally completed. We stop to climb into the trunk of a gnarled old tree and then it's all down hill. Bouncing on bikes over ruts and skidding in the gravel of Milk Ranch Road, we slow for uphill hikers and downhill horses and come full circle 15 miles to the trout pond where we began.

Our laboring over, I think of the miners toiling underground searching for gold in Julian and Cuyamaca City. Now in the fall the gold can be found in the California Black Oak leaves and in the fir, cedar and pine forests preserved for all.

Conditions have changed since the Cedar Fire destroyed a substantial portion of Cuyamaca Rancho Park. I have left the Grand Loop and Oakzanita bike trips as they were

Aftermath of the Cedar Fire, Cuyamaca Rancho

written prior to the fire as a record of what Cuyamaca Rancho Park had been.

Postscript: November 29, 2003

When we arrive in Julian, the streets are packed with people. The historic downtown had been saved from the worst fire in San Diego history. Steven L. Rucker, a Novato firefighter, had lost his life in the fire assisting southern California firefighters. Many had lost homes, crops, barns and personal property. Yet, the Julian News headline read: SIGNS OF HOPE.

We joined the crowds eating comforting apple pie then with trepidation drove out Highway 79 toward Cuyamaca Rancho Park.

At Lake Cuyamaca anglers fished for trout and bass; ducks swam in the lake. We continued on and it didn't look so bad really at first. But on the ridge overlooking the lake, we could see that only 25 out of 145 homes were still standing as reported. Chimneys and foundations stood alone—the homes burned to the ground. It seemed as if a nuclear bomb or some terrible blast had gone off on the ridge.

We continued down Highway 79 and utility service crews waved us around the detour where they worked to replace telephone poles. Then with agony we began to witness the wildfire's elemental power of destruction. Mile by mile, frame by frame, the forest became a grainy black and white horror film. It was like looking at Ansel Adams black and white photographs of the ridges, trees and boulders. Ancient oak trees resembled drift wood, sculptural shapes with uplifted arms. Oaks have thick bark to protect them from fire but could any of them survive? What about all the chaparral and coastal sage scrub? Gray ash now replaced all the undergrowth.

What bitter irony—the Dyer family home used as a visitor center is in shambles but just across the highway a manzanita bush stands with green foliage. We drove on naively hoping Oakzanita Peak had been spared. T.M. broke the rules and pulled over. There is no stopping in the park allowed. I photographed the Peak, now a skeleton with all the flesh burned off.

We dropped down into Descanso past melted white fences and scorched boulders. A very special San Diego park was gone and we felt as if we had been to a funeral.

As I was taking pictures I told T.M., "We will come back every year and record the new Cuyamaca Rancho Park that will be restored." But back at home the image of a grayscale snapshot of one of the burned ridges with treetops burned off into sharp pointed sticks and white ash covering the ground haunted me. I thought about the raven's call the last time we had picnicked outside the visitor center under the oak trees. Would Cuyamaca be "*Nevermore?*"

Hope came in the form of a picture and another newspaper headline. *The Los Angeles Times* article by Thomas Curwen was titled "A rare Survivor." Seems 20-30 rare Cuyamaca cypress trees were still alive!

Fire is essential to the plants and trees of southern California. The heat and smoke of a wildfire send a signal to seeds to germinate. Fewer trees mean more sunlight for seeds to grow.

Mike Evans, the owner of the *Tree of Life Nursery*, lost a brand new cabin on North Peak in Cuyamaca in the Cedar

Fire. He, as a specialist in native California plants and trees, said oaks may appear dead but leaves and branches may sprout from old wood! He estimated a robust recovery of the coastal sage scrub and chaparral in 5-10 years. Woodlands would require 10-15 years while mountain evergreen forests needed 20-30 years for new immature stands to be established. As for a healthy forest teeming with wildlife it may be another 30-50 years. But it won't be until 2104 that the forest may look like old growth. Perhaps the raven was wrong after all.

~ Travel Notes ~

Julian is 60 miles northeast of San Diego along Highway 78. From the north, take Interstate 15 south to State Highway 79 east at Temecula. From downtown San Diego take I-8 east to State Highway 79 north 22 miles to Julian. It is approximately 12.6 miles north on Highway 79 to the trout pond where we start the Grand Loop Trail.

The Eagle/High Peak Mine Tour is in Julian one-quarter mile east up "C" St. Admission fees: Adults $8, children $4, under 5 $1. The tour is very professional and worth the trip. Picnic area available for tour guests.

Due to the catastrophic Cedar Fire in October 2003 conditions in Cuyamaca Rancho may have changed.

Another great place to hike is The Volcan Mountain Wilderness Preserve. It is open 7 days a week from dawn to dusk for a 3 mile roundtrip hike. From Julian, take Farmer Road 2.2 miles, turn right on Wynola Road for about 100 yards, then turn left, back onto the continuation of Farmer Road. Proceed a short distance and park on the shoulder of the paved road by the Preserve sign on the right side of road. Hike starts at the intriguing gateway created by James Hubbel. Docent guided 5 mile roundtrip hikes to the top are offered once a month. Web site www.volcanmt.org

From Julian to Cuyamaca Rancho State Park, take Highway 79 south 9.5 miles passing Lake Cuyamaca and continuing south a short distance to the trout pond parking area on the left across from the Boy Scout camp.

To reach the Stonewall Peak Mine from this parking area, proceed 0.6 miles on Highway 79 and go left on the paved Los Vaqueros Road. Approximately 1 mile up this road make another left. The Stonewall Mine is 0.2 mile up the road. There is a 0.6 mile trail circling around the mine site. There is a shaded picnic area with grills and picnic tables.

To continue on the Grand Loop Trail return back 0.2 mile to the T and go straight 0.2 mile through a cattle fence to the narrow dirt trail on the left. Starting on the Grand Loop dirt trail off Los Vaqueros, proceed 1 mile up to a T. Then make a left and go 0.9 mile to a saddle, then 0.8 mile down Soapstone Grade Fire Road. At the bottom turn right and go down Green Valley Fire Road 3.1 miles to Park headquarters. There are shaded picnic tables here. (Return the way you came if you desire to shorten the ride.)

From Park headquarters, ride up to Highway 79 and turn left heading south 1.1 miles to the Trail on your right. Go north on Japacha/West Mesa Fire Road 1.4 miles. Turn left on Fern Flat Fire Road. Go north 5.5 miles crossing paved Lookout Road. Continue another 1.4 miles down to a T. Go right on Milk Ranch Road down 1.7 miles to Highway 79 and the Parking area at the trout pond.

Grand Loop Trail Mix

We ride the Grand Loop for my birthday every year. When T.M. bonked at the start of the climbing the Medjools gave him instant energy to finish the ride.

Combine 1/3 cup each of:
Walnuts
Dried cranberries
Raisins
Add whole Medjool Dates as desired.

Pack in baggy for the trail.

Trail of Oakzanita

Mountain bike the Oakzanita Trail, Rancho Cuyamaca State Park,
Melodrama at the Julian Town Hall

A

Pine Nut Cookies

On the TRAIL OF OAKZANITA, we park at the East
Mesa Fire Road trailhead. Early morning breezes and
a gradual uphill ride keep us cool and pedaling easily with oak
tree branches arching above. The "zanita" part of the trail

name comes from the prolific
Eastwood, Cuyamaca and
Mexican manzanita shrubs
growing on the dry hillsides of
the Park.

One great reward of
mountain biking in San Diego
is pedaling through groves of
oak trees. From many other
rides I have a series of pictures
of my yellow bike in the
foreground of pictures of
golden broadleafed oak trees.

Every curve I round, I see
a photo opportunity with the
dappled sun shining through
the brown and gold leaves of

Oakzanita Trail

California Black Oaks.
Though I know I will get way behind T.M., I dismount and
place my yellow Specialized hard-tail bike near the black trunk
and take several photos. Before pushing off again, I turn and
look toward the coast. A thick marine layer smothers it like a
black pillow.

177

Happy to be up in the sun, I find T.M. has waited. After just under three miles of moderate climbing we are at the junction where a right turn takes the single track Trail to the summit of Oakzanita Peak. This section of the Trail has recently been opened to mountain bikers. We forego the fun and technical climb to the top to continue straight to a favorite picnic spot under an ancient oak.

While pedaling through a meadow, I laugh to myself thinking about the Julian Melodrama we had seen the night before at the Julian Town hall. It was opening night and the cast, the play and first night bloopers had us laughing all the way to the end of the funny, professional performance called the *Stalwart Surveyor*.

"Curses!! Foiled Again!" The villain, Desmond Delancy, a giant of a man in a black stovepipe hat, twirled his handlebar moustache then drew his black cape over his face as he exited the stage. "Boooo!!! Hiss!!!" The audience taunted.

Sweet Amanda was in danger of being lured away from the hero, Archibald Gimlet. "Don't go with Desmond! Don't get into the carriage!" We shouted warnings to her. She didn't listen and took Mr. Delancy's arm. If Archibald doesn't return to save his fiancée what will happen to her and what will happen to the miners of Cuyamaca? Of course, before the play ends our heroine was rescued from the clutches of evil Delancy and the miners of Cuyamaca held their gold claims.

Outside the theatre the cast had greeted us. I said, "Bravo, you are a great villain, Mr. Delancy."

"Why yes," he said. "We all have some villain in us!"

No scoundrels up here on this easy route, just a rendezvous with a favorite tree. After about 50 minutes of pedaling we reach the enormous oak. It might take four or more people with clasped hands to encircle the trunk. Its mantle of leaves protects us from the sun. A leisurely picnic under the oak's sprawling umbrella and then it is time for cruising downhill fast but always with special consideration for hikers, uphill bikers and especially horseback riders sharing the Trail.

"Meet you at the car," TM speeds away from the old tree and me. I'm reluctant to leave the place where this oak graced the landscape. Places like this help us keep our moorings and balance but it is time to reap the gift of biking. The sweet reward of the downhill is made sweeter by Bob Dylan's song, *It's All Over Now, Baby Blue* playing over and over in my head.

~ Travel Notes ~

Due to the catastrophic Cedar Fire in October 2003 Cuyamaca Rancho State Park conditions may have changed. I have left the Grand Loop and Oakzanita bike trips as they were written prior to the fire as a record of what Cuyamaca Rancho Park had been.

Cuyamaca Rancho State Park is 40 miles east of San Diego along Highway 79. From the north take Interstate 15 south to State Highway 79 east at Temecula. Or from downtown San Diego take I-8 east to State Highway 79 north.

The Oakzanita Trail starts at the East Mesa Fire Road parking area off Highway 79, south of Cuyamaca Rancho State Park headquarters at mile marker 3.5. It is a moderate 2.8 miles of climbing to the fork in the Trail. Go right to climb the 5,054-foot Oakzanita Peak now open to bikers or continue straight ahead for a mostly level roll through the meadow to the oak tree. Return the way you came. Watch for hikers and horses.

The Julian Melodrama plays at the Julian town hall on weekends in October. Well worth attending!

Pine Nut Cookies

Kumeyaay Indians parched and roasted the nuts of the Pinyon Pine.

1 cup butter
¾ cup firmly packed brown sugar
2 eggs
½ cup stone ground white cornmeal
1 cup white flour
6 ounces pine nuts, coarsely chopped

Preheat oven to 325°.

Cream butter and sugar together until light. Beat in eggs one at a time. Mix together cornmeal and flour. Stir in gradually. Mix in pine nuts.

Drop heaping tablespoons of dough onto cookie sheets, pressing lightly to flatten. Cookies will be done when edges begin to brown about 10 minutes. Cool completely on racks.

Trail of the Laguna Mountains

Laguna Mountain Visitor Center at Mount Laguna,
hike the Sunset Trail to Water of the Woods

ᚠ

Sunset Trail Chocolate Chip Cookies

The Sunrise Highway leads us to the lush meadows and woods of the Laguna Mountains in the Cleveland National Forest. On the TRAIL OF THE LAGUNA MOUNTAINS we pop into the Laguna Visitor Information office to purchase a current Adventure Pass. The Ranger suggests that if we are hiking the Sunset Trail we can make a loop route passing Water of the Woods.

Sunset Trail

At three o'clock we start up the Trail. I decide to leave my tape recorder running to capture the experience. This hike begins in a meadow filled with the sweet essence of vanilla, the signature scent of a Jeffrey Pine. Only the savory Coastal Sagebrush of the coastal foothills and the sweet desert Creosote Bush in my opinion rivals this refreshing aroma. I had assumed the five-inch long bunched needles produced the pine intoxicant but the aroma actually comes from the creases in the bark on the trunk.

Sunset Trail

Also in the meadow are clumps of leafless California Black Oak trees. Closer examination reveals tiny green buds. The oaks will have gorgeous seven-lobed leaves that turn gold in the fall. Stellar Jays shrill *shaack shaack shack* at us as we cross under their nests perched 10 to 100 feet above us in the trees. Western Scrub Jays and California Gray Squirrels are important to the future of the oak woodland. Of the hundreds of acorns they bury for food, some grow into oak trees.

Kwaaymii Indians

If it were a fall day centuries ago, we might hear the cracking of acorns with rounded stones by the Kwaaymii, a band of the Kumeyaay Indians inhabiting the Laguna Mountains. They gathered, shelled and dried the large prized acorns.

I tell T.M. that the Indian women used to hide their favorite stone pestles in the holes of trees and at harvest time would find them again before going to a favorite grinding rock to pound the acorns into a coarse flour. The meal made a fine tasting dish called *shawii* but the bitter taste of the tannin had to be leached out first.

Water of the Woods

After about 20 minutes of easy level hiking and bird scoldings, we reach Water of the Woods. But in this drought year it looks more like Puddle of the Woods.

The Laguna Mountain meadows lush with grass and plentiful water were perfect for Californio cattle ranching in the 1800s. In 1849, the California gold

Water of the Woods

rush kept cattle ranchers busy raising beef for miners in
northern California.

We take the rangers advice and climb the ridge above
Water of the Woods and divert toward the Big Laguna Trail.
Tracks in the mud of the earthen wall around the water show
signs of earlier visitors. Mountain lions, bobcats and deer come
to drink from Water of the Woods. Our rhythmic footsteps and
stab of hiking sticks follow along their departing tracks on the
Sunset Trail toward Big Laguna. An unidentified bird calls *pu
pu peep peep peep peep*. Wind roars wildly up the ravine and
rushes through treetops. Viewed from above, the elliptical blue
pool of Water of the Woods swirls with yellow-green pond
scum.

If we continued to the end of the Sunset Trail going this
direction we would wind up at the junction with Big Laguna
Trail, a favorite mountain bike and hiking trail.

Big Laguna Trail

This trail is named for the Lake formed in the meadow by
snowmelt and winter rains. Last fall while riding the Big
Laguna Trail, we had observed an area reserved for a special
black and white butterfly but couldn't recall its name. The
ranger today informed us the pine forest habitat is set aside for
the Laguna Mountain Skipper butterfly.

"Have any been seen?"

"No. The plants it needs grow there but someone sat up
there for three years looking with no success. Now that's a
boring job."

"Sitting in a forest for years, I might volunteer for that duty."

The same day we had mountain biked the Big Laguna
Trail, we picnicked near a mysterious tree by the Penny Pines
parking area. The old tree drilled with thousands of holes had
been stuffed with acorns. Curious to learn by whom or what, I
happened upon an article in the Cuyamaca Rancho State
newspaper about the remarkable habits of the "carpenter of
acorns," the Acorn Woodpecker.

The Carpenter of the Acorns

The Acorn Woodpecker has a "super-cushioned" skull that allows drilling into hardwood without getting a migraine as it fills the tree, called a granary, with acorns for future food.

Chacup chacup chacup is its call but more likely you will hear the subtle tat tat tat on the trunk of a tree. White eyes surrounded by black and a red cap on the head give the bird a Kachina doll face. In flight, patches on wings flash white against the trees making them fairly easy to spot.

Today, after a total of 45 minutes of hiking, we top out at 5,500 feet on the Sunset Trail before it drops down to Big Laguna. At this high vista point, we rest in the shade of tall manzanita before going back to Water of the Woods. Oakzanita Peak is a small bump to the south and Cuyamaca Peak is to our west.

Back at Water of the Woods

Red-winged Blackbirds sit atop cattails calling *okaleee okaleee* as we cross to the other side of Water of the Woods on the loop of Sunset Trail heading back toward the car. We flush a gobbling and yelping wild turkey into a tree. One last whiff of the heaven scent of the pines and we finish the trail in two hours.

We clean up, change clothes and go straight to dinner at Japango's in La Jolla to meet a friend just in from Texas. We tell him about our hike of the Sunset Trail. He expected it must be a faraway place and was surprised to hear we were less than an hour from La Jolla.

"That's why I love coming to San Diego! The diversity is incredible!"

Later that week, I rewound and listened to my tape with anticipation of reliving the trail experience. My rhythmic footsteps sounded like an elephant crashing along the trail. I did capture the songs of birds I knew: a jay scolding and a quail's laugh. And some birds I couldn't identify and didn't remember hearing at the time.

Did I capture the wind? Yes, if wind and static have anything in common. Fun to listen to, the tape did run capture the essence of the hike. I couldn't smell the pines or feel the wind. That is why the Trail calls us back over and over to engage all of our senses.

~ Travel Notes ~

From San Diego take Interstate 5 to Interstate 8 east to Sunrise Highway. Go north 5.3 miles to Sunset Trailhead.

To reach the Laguna Mountain Recreation Area Information Center from Julian drive south on Highway 79 for 6 miles. Take a left turn onto Sunrise Highway (S1) and proceed 14.6 miles to Mount Laguna near mile marker 23. Or proceed north from Sunset Trailhead 4.5 miles. An Adventure Pass for parking in the National forest can be purchased at the Visitor Center as well as maps. Adventure Pass fee: day pass $5, annual pass $30 and a second annual pass purchased at same time $5, (great for gifts) available at the Laguna Mountain Visitor Center open Friday, Saturday and Sunday.

The Sunset Trailhead is 4.5 miles farther south on the Sunrise Highway close to the Meadows Information Center near mile marker 19.5. You must display the Adventure Pass on parked vehicles.

To follow the loop route we took, about 100 yards up the Trail, take the right fork toward Water of the Woods. Cross the earthen dam and continue north up the ridge above the Water. Go as far as you like. We stopped at the high point at an elevation of 5,798 feet then returned and crossed back to the other side of Water of the Woods and followed the Sunset Trail back to the car.

Several of our favorite picnic spots are: under the oaks trees at mile marker 29 at the Pioneer Mail Trailhead area, and around Penny Pines parking area at mile marker 27 where a short walk brings sweeping views to the depths of the Anza-Borrego desert below. Look for the Acorn Woodpecker granary tree on the west side of the road.

Sunset Trail Chocolate Chip Cookies

A flavor nearly as heavenly as the delicious vanilla scent of the Laguna Jeffrey Pines

4½ cups flour
2 teaspoons baking soda
2 teaspoons kosher salt or big grain* sea salt
2 cups butter (4 sticks)
1 cup sugar
2 cups brown sugar
4 teaspoons vanilla
4 eggs
1-2 cups bittersweet chocolate chips

Preheat oven to 375°.

Sift together flour, soda and salt in a small bowl.

In a large bowl combine softened butter, sugars and vanilla. Beat until creamy. Beat eggs into mixture one at a time. Stir in flour mixture gradually and add chocolate chips.

Drop by heaping teaspoons onto cookie sheets. Bake for 9-11 minutes until tops are golden. Let stand on cookie sheets for several minutes then place on cooling racks.

Makes about 8 dozen cookies.

 * Using big grain sea salt gives the crunch of the salt grains with the bite of the bittersweet chocolate.

Trail of Borrego Palm Canyon

*Hike the Borrego Palm Canyon Trail in Anza-Borrego Desert
State Park and stop at Visitor Center*

☍

Susan's Snickerdoodle Cookies

W hen we visited the Adagio Gallery in Palm Springs
yesterday the last thing we intended to do was buy a
painting. The artist Miguel Martinez "hailed as one of the
great living Latino American artists today" was showing his
striking portraits of Latina women and landscapes of the
Southwest. Inspired by Miguel's work, we bought one of his
prints called *Time*. He told us he had used pastels to hand-
color the sky, the plants, the mountains and the faces of
the women.

Today we head from Palm Springs out to the Anza-
Borrego Desert on the TRAIL OF BORREGO PALM
CANYON. From Palm Springs, we swing out to Indio, pass the
town of Coachella and head toward the Salton Sea with the
painting bundled in the back of the truck. Soon the Sea
glistens to the east and at Salton City we turn west toward the
mountains and Anza-Borrego State Park in San Diego County.

Anza-Borrego Desert State Park

As we travel into the Park with the new picture in mind, I
see a Martinez landscape sketched and colored with an artist's
hand; the deep olive-green of the creosote bush leaves, the red
flames of the spring ocotillo flowers and the watery blue sky.
Burnt umber washes over the San Ysidro and Laguna Canyon
Mountains holding back a massive white cloudbank keeping
the desert dry.

Wind generated from a passing cold Pacific storm whips up around us. Knowing the popularity of this trail, we opt to drive the short distance from the Visitor Center to the Campground to get a jumpstart on the Sunday hiking crowd. Two helpful park volunteers stationed at the trailhead ask a vital desert question: "Got water?"

We point to our camelback water packs that also contain extra clothes and food even though this is only a three-mile hike out and back. T.M. grabs a self-guiding trail brochure and we are off.

Borrego Palm Canyon Trail

Drought conditions prevailed this winter. Normal rainfall by now would have been five to six inches. A wildflower hotline recording had said only 1.5 inches of rain so far. Still, this tiny amount of moisture brought forth modest displays of red flowers and emerald leaves to the stalks of the Ocotillo.

T.M. snaps a close-up shot with snaky canes waving over my head like Medusa. We stop to crush desert lavender and are rewarded by a pungent pleasing aroma.

It has been a decade since we had first hiked the Borrego Canyon Trail. Yet every step I take seems as if it were yesterday. We remembered on that morning long ago we had seen bighorn sheep come down to the Campground for water. T.M. says we need to keep a good eye out for them today.

My ears start to ache from the piercing wind. I pull up my hood and trudge up the desert wash. T.M. stops to peer into the desert willows, which are not true willows at all, deeply rooted they survive arid conditions and little rain. He has seen the flash of blue bird in the thicket and is trying to figure out what kind it is.

As luck would have it, a man with binoculars and bird book in hand strides toward us. From our description he identifies our bird as a Blue-gray Gnatcatcher. He points out a Black-throated Sparrow perched nearby. As we talk an unseen bird whistles descending notes "tew tew tew tew tew."

"Canyon Wren," the bird expert cocks his ear and smiles listening to the bird's downslurred notes whistled like drops of water falling. His book shows the Canyon Wren's color as a brown and gray body with white throat and breast and a very long bill for swooping up insects and spiders. Thanking the generous man we resume our climb up the rocky trail.

Earlier in the week, I had been listening to Edward Abbey's lauded book, *Desert Solitaire*, on tape. In his recollection of his days as a park ranger at Arches National Monument, he wrote of the song of the Canyon Wrens. Now I had heard one. I wonder if Edward Abbey is still alive and writing about the Southwestern desert he loved? Born in 1927, I hope he is.

On a stop at number 15 on our guide, we gaze out one-half mile into the distance to a bright-green palm oasis. The Desert Fanpalm, the only palm native to California, symbolized life to desert travelers and the Indians. It was a sign of a permanent water source.

The Palm Oasis

After 50 minutes of easy hiking we reach the palms. The heart of the oasis is barricaded. Seems people have been coming here at the rate of 50,000 a year and that makes for a lot of trampling on the little upstart seedlings. Seated on a large rock, I sketch the double waterfall. Two streams of water rush around a big boulder with a soothing swoosh.

The Cahuilla and Kumeyaay Indians camped here. The oasis provided the

Borrego Palm Oasis

village with respite from the burning sun and a permanent source of water. The Cahuilla used palm thatch to fashion clothing and build a shelter called a "kish." Intricate baskets of palm fibers and sacred objects were made of the dried fronds. The rocks show evidence of the tedious grinding of mesquite beans and palm seeds by ancient women in centuries past.

Desert Varnish

Glad I don't have to do any of that grinding work, I sit down on the warm rock and examine the darkened reddish-brown color of the boulders, which our paper guide says took 10,000 years to paint. The striking brown color of the "rock varnish" is thought to be the result of colonies of bacteria that absorb manganese and iron from the air then attach tiny bits of clay to themselves to stay moist.

On a rock outcrop above the oasis I pull out our picnic lunch. Wind shakes and shivers the palm fronds. They shimmer like ocean waves. Hummingbirds buzz our heads. My fleece coat feels good.

We retrace our steps passing many people coming up the Trail. "Does it get more difficult?" they ask. "Have you seen any bighorn sheep?"

Just over two hours from our start we stand back at the trailhead looking at darting pupfish in the Campground pond. The cold wind and poor showing of flowers has driven most campers home. The ramadas stand empty except for mice scurrying for leftover crumbs.

Visitor Center

Inside the quiet stone structure of the Visitor Center, I learn the rain shadow effect—why it is dry here in the desert and drizzling at the beach. When moist ocean air is channeled inland, the mountain peaks act as barriers obstructing the flow of coastal air. As the air mass approaches the high peaks, the moisture in the air rises, cools and condenses. The effect on the desert side of the mountain is the billowing white clouds seemingly stuck on the peaks. The moisture has been wrung out of the clouds.

We thumb the excellent selection of books and maps on the desert. Then, I spot Edward Abbey's *Desert Solitaire* on the shelf. The back cover reads, "Died in 1989 in Oracle, Arizona." A little saddened by this revelation, we leave the stonewalled fortress for our truck with our blanket-wrapped treasure.

At home we hang the *Martinez* on the living room wall. Each time I pass the two silent beautiful women with their stunning eyes, I think of another place, the seductive Anza-Borrego desert, where the landscape is sketched and mountains, flowers and skies are hand-colored.

~ Travel Notes ~

From Interstate 5 exit at Highway 76 in Oceanside. Go east on Highway 76 for 69 miles. Or from Interstate 15 go east 51.5 miles. When Highway 76 ends, turn left onto Highway 79 and continue on for about 5 miles to S-2. Turn right on S-2 and go approximately 5 miles to Highway S-22. Turn left on Highway S-22 passing through the small town of Ranchita and down a 12-mile grade. At the stop sign turn left to the Visitor Center. (It is about a 2 hour drive from San Diego or Palm Springs.)

Anza-Borrego Desert State Park is at 200 Palm Canyon Drive in Borrego Springs. www.anzaborrego.statepark.org

The Visitor Center is open October through May daily from 9 a.m. to 5 p.m. June through September open weekends and holidays only.

The Borrego Palm Canyon trailhead is at the campground, 6/10 of a mile from the Visitor Center.

Susan's Snickerdoodle Cookies

1 cup butter
1½ cups sugar
2 eggs
2¾ cups flour
2 teaspoons cream of tartar
1 teaspoon baking soda
½ teaspoon salt
Sugar and cinnamon

Mix together butter, sugar and eggs. Add flour, cream of tartar, soda and salt. Chill for at least 2 hours.

Roll into balls the size of walnuts. Roll in sugar and cinnamon mixture. Bake on an ungreased cookie sheet at 400° for 8-10 minutes.

Makes several dozen.

Trail of Hellhole Canyon

*Hike up Hellhole Canyon to Maidenhair Falls in
Anza-Borrego Desert State Park*

꠸

Hellhole Turkey Chili

Hellhole Canyon. The Anza-Borrego wildflower hotline buzzed with the news! A glorious wildflower show in the canyon: Lupine, Trixis, Filaree, Ocotillo, Rock Daisy, Bladderpod, Desert Apricot, California Buckwheat, Desert Trumpet, Desert Rock Pea, Beavertail Cactus and Thick-leaved Ground Cherry.

Anxious to get to the Canyon before the blooming season ended, we hit the TRAIL OF HELLHOLE CANYON at 8:30 a.m. on a Sunday in March armed with *Wildflowers of Anza-Borrego* and a 35 mm camera. Just a few giant steps up the primitive road the flower show begins.

The hot-pink blossoms of the Beavertail Cactus resemble Mexican paper flowers. The Beavertail is one of the easier cacti to remember with its distinctive bluish-gray paddles sporting small clustered spines called glochids.

A young couple wrangles with their toddler squatting down to touch the magenta flower on the clustered spiked stems of an Englemann Hedgehog. I snap photos of the yellow blooms of Buckhorn Cholla. After fumbling with the wildflower identifier brochure, I can identify the frenzy of red tubular flowers on an almost leafless shrub as Chuparosa.

The Ocotillo

I run to catch up with T.M., who is now long gone. But it is hard to keep my feet moving for more than a few steps. I run straight into a splendid old 15-foot ocotillo in full spring dress;

193

multiple canes thick with emerald leaves shooting up into the sky. Tight clusters of sunset-red flowers bloom at the end of each cane. However, thorns lurk below this beguiling cover. Despite the spines, it is not a cactus.

On other hikes I have heard the language of the black carpenter bees visiting the ocotillos in the heavy silence of the rocky slopes. Today the bees don't speak.

George Wharton James

Few plants of the desert elicit such admiration as the ocotillo. George Wharton James, turn-of-the-century photographer and writer, wrote: "Sometimes, when looking toward the sun, the flower appears like a brilliantly feathered bird resting on the end of the limb."

Edmund Jaeger

Edmund Jaeger, botanist and world-renowned desert authority, wrote in 1940 that he thought the ocotillo was a plant of extraordinary vigor. Seldom had he seen a dead cane although he noted windstorms could flatten the plant.

The Desert Fanpalm Oasis

Finally, nearly two-thirds of the way up the trail to our destination, Maidenhair Falls, I catch up to T.M. standing on a boulder bird watching. A California quail, our state bird, forages for seeds on the ground crying a three-note "chi-ca-

Ocotillo in full spring dress

go." T.M. points out a Scott's Oriole with flashing yellow belly and wing patch contrasted on a black body and head. I tell T.M. I have read that orioles like the red flowers of the ocotillo and so do warblers and humbles. The plants also serves us a main food source for hummingbirds migrating north from Mexico to the mountains of the West.

The sculptural sycamore trees with their large star-shaped leaves and rustling cottonwood trees alive to any touch of the breeze, share the water of the Desert Fanpalms. We know our destination, Maidenhair Falls, is getting close.

Sweat soaks our clothes as the scramble up the rocks takes us away from the cooling oasis. Yellow butterflies light on the rocks and an army caterpillar wriggles by.

Maidenhair Falls

Finally we reach the Falls. Removing his sunglasses T.M. stares into the cool grotto shaded by gigantic boulders and overhanging tangle of growth. The damp desert hideaway provides a surprise!

"Look at this!"

Poking my head inside I see delicate ferns growing on the wet slippery rock.

"What kind are they?" T.M. asks.

"Fiddlehead, I think they are fiddlehead ferns."

Red-faced, we cool down in the shade of a boulder outside.

"Here," I say to T.M., spreading out dates, almonds, and apples and handing him a sandwich, "This is the best sandwich you'll ever eat." Of course, any trail food tastes good and especially when the hike's destination has been reached.

When we descend to the thatch-strewn Palm Oasis two hikers ask,"Did you see the Maidenhair Ferns?"

Like dunces we hadn't even connected the ferns that we had just seen to the name of the Falls. They informed us it was indeed a rare treat to see them this year. Seems they don't always appear unless the conditions are just right.

Now people stream up the primitive road. Most have no water and are dressed in sandals and wearing their clean Sunday-best clothes.

"How far to the wildflowers?"

"Not far. Not far at all."

I know that if we were to return to this Trail after a rainless month or so, the ocotillo's green leaves would have turned yellow and dropped; the once brilliant flowers strewn on the ground would be dusty and brown. The gray sticks of the dormant ocotillo would have to wait again for that infrequent, sustaining rain.

Back home I discover there are hundreds of varieties of ferns and that a "fiddlehead" is just the name for the young coiled frond of a fern. I also learn there are at least four other Hellhole Canyons in the United States.

Do hellish place names given to canyons like these dupe travelers into thinking they are places that are to be avoided, thus preserve them? Or had Hellhole been cursed by a traveler with parched waterless tongue on a searing hot day with the sun wheeling mercilessly overhead? Seek out these destinations. When you least expect it a journey may reveal unexpected and rare heavenly beauty, especially if you go to Hellhole Canyon.

~ Travel Notes ~

From Interstate 5 exit at Highway 76 in Oceanside. Go east on Highway 76 for 69 miles. Or from Interstate 15 go east 51.5 miles. When Highway 76 ends, turn left onto Highway 79 and continue on for about 5 miles to S-2. Turn right on S-2 and go approximately 5 miles to Highway S-22. Turn left on Highway S-22 passing through the small town of Ranchita and down a 12-mile grade. At the stop sign turn left to the Visitor Center. (It is about a 2 hour drive from San Diego or Palm Springs.)

Anza-Borrego Desert State Park is at 200 Palm Canyon Drive in Borrego Springs. www.anzaborrego.statepark.org

The Visitor Center is open October through May daily from 9 a.m. to 5 p.m. June through September open weekends and holidays only.

To get to Hellhole Canyon trailhead from the Visitor Center, drive south on S-22 .7 miles to the Hellhole Parking lot on your right. This is a moderately difficult, 6-mile roundtrip hike with some rock scrambling necessary to reach the Falls. The wide Trail heads up the alluvial fan and eventually narrows at the mouth of the canyon.

Hellhole Turkey Chili

2 lbs. ground turkey
1 green bell pepper, chopped
2 yellow bell pepper, chopped
1 large red onion, chopped
3-4 cloves of garlic, minced
4 Serrano chilies, seeded and diced (or more to taste)
1 bunch of cilantro, chopped
One 12-oz. can of kidney Beans
One 12-oz. can of pinto Beans
One 12-oz. can of chili Beans
One 12-oz. can of tomato paste
Two 14-oz. cans of Mexican stewed tomatoes
One 28-oz. can of chopped tomatoes
Two 12-oz. cans of chicken broth
1 tablespoon ground cumin
2-3 tablespoons chili Powder to taste
1 Tablespoon salt, to taste

Spray large pot with cooking spray. Brown onion, peppers, and garlic. About halfway browned, add turkey and 1 Tbs. of chili powder. When the turkey is browned, add the rest of the ingredients (including liquid) and simmer 2 hours.

Trail of Elephant Knees to Elephant Trees

Hike to the top of the Elephant Knees and short loop hike along the Elephant Tree Discovery Trail in Anza-Borrego Desert State Park

뀨
Smoked Turkey Sandwich

Pink and beige sheer walls rise hundreds of feet above us on both sides of the Fish Creek gorge. We are bound for the TRAIL OF THE ELEPHANT KNEES AND THE ELEPHANT TREES bumping along Split Mountain Road in the southeastern section of the Anza-Borrego Desert. The unusual names bestowed upon these desert trails add to our anticipation. Just what do Elephant's Knees look like? How will we recognize an Elephant tree?

We lace up boots, grasp walking sticks and sprint into the Mud Hills Wash. The prehistoric desert welcomes and stuns us with an absolute overwhelming silence broken only by the pop-pop crunch of mud curls breaking like china under our lug-soled boots. A child-like pleasure comes over me in this action like popping bubble wrap or seaweed bulbs on the beach.

"We're on the rim of the Fish Creek Badlands now." T.M. proclaims.

Borrego Valley Inn

Yesterday we had booked a room at the Borrego Valley Inn in the small friendly town of Borrego Springs to celebrate our twentieth wedding anniversary. We arrived at "magic time" and camera in hand I captured photos of the dark brown San Ysidro Mountains backlit by the golden sun before sundown. I turned the lens to the Inn's tinkling fountain and courtyard aviary where little white birds welcomed us with high-pitched *chee-chee* calls.

No green grass or tropical plants here. Native desert plants like Creosote Bushes bobbed and trimmed into poodle-cut topiaries set the stage. Desert mallow shot up orange blooms and scarlet fairy dusters painted the square red. We called a hiking friend and raved, "The adobe-style Inn looks more like a movie set in New Mexico than in San Diego County." She sighed with envy at our good fortune to be hiking in Anza Borrego in wild flower season.

Palms at Indian Head

As the final minutes of magic time faded away, we made a beeline for dinner at the Krazy Coyote Salon and Grille in the historic Palms at Indian Head. The Old Hoberg Resort was the first major resort in Borrego Springs. Burned down, rebuilt and restored again, the newest incarnation is a lovely glass-walled two-story lodge.

Twilight cast heavy blue-gray shadows on the pale blue water in the Olympic-size swimming pool as we settled in our chairs on the patio. In the heydays of the 1950s, Hollywood stars Will Rodgers, Bing Crosby, Clark Gable and Marilyn Monroe sat in the same twilight in the shadow of Indian Head Mountain. The sweetly-scented wind swayed the lacy fronds of the date palm trees framing our view of the desert beyond. I said to T.M., "It's different in Borrego Springs. The primitive desert is still out there."

Back at the Borrego Valley Inn, the birds in the aviary were asleep. Magic time was now star time. And before we went to sleep we sat in the courtyard and gazed up at the black sky, silver stars and the Milky Way for a long time.

At five o'clock this morning, I propped myself up on one elbow to witness first light on the San Ysidro Mountains. Our waitress at the Palms had recommended Kendall's Cafe in the downtown mall. We mulled over our many hiking choices while we wolfed down delicious pancakes and drank cups of tea. We had settled on a hike called the Elephant Knees and drove from downtown Borrego Springs to Ocotillo Wells and turned off at Split Mountain Road.

Split Mountain Road

Split Mountain road divides the Vallecito Mountains on our left from the Fish Creek Mountains on our right. A Park sign explains this is the Split Mountain Fault zone and that floodwater cut down through the layered rock to create Fish Creek. Thousands of tons of debris caught in raging flash flood waters plummet through Split Mountain cutting out the deep gorge. The gorge provides an outlet for fallen rock that has existed in the Fault Zone for over 20 million years. The powerful floodwaters surge from here another 20 miles to the Salton Sea.

I took a photo of T.M. sitting in the Sequoia by the roadside. The surrounding walls made our Sport Utility Vehicle look like a Hot Wheel toy.

Nearing the Fish Creek campground the fantastic folded walls—the narrow gaps—the extraordinary cliffs remind me of the remains of an ancient walled city.

Mud Hills Wash

Anxious to get out on foot, we finally spot the Oyster Shell Reef information panel where the unmaintained hiking trail to the Elephant's Knees begins. Here we learn this Oyster Shell Reef once was the undersea realm of Gulf of California.

T.M. bends down to pick up

T.M. winds up the wash toward the Elephant Knees

201

something. "This is what glints in the sun, they're embedded in the mud hills. Gypsum crystals and oyster shells."

Elephant Knees

We round the Mud Hill bend. Gray crinkled tapered stumpy limbs rise up to a plateau before us. The Elephant Knees are aptly named and resemble a row of the lower limbs of five-toed pachyderms. It's not magic time but still early enough to get good definition on the knees with my camera before the shadowless, unmerciful afternoon sun obscures all detail.

Our hike destination is to get to the backside of the "Knees" and climb to the top of the long, narrow mesa top. Keeping the Knees to our right shoulders, we wind around to the back of the beast. T.M. picks a good spot to bushwhack up, mindful that we walk on top of a 12-15 foot deep Oyster Shell Reef that two million years ago was part of the Gulf of California.

Fish Creek Badlands

We quickly reach the narrow precipice. Hearts pound as we steady ourselves for a look-around the Fish Creek Wash. Using binoculars, T.M. points out the Wind Caves, another hike in the Fish Creek region we could do today. The Fish Creek badland sediments are rounded and humpy like soft yellow suede pillows. And I could use a pillow right now as we picnic on the sharp, hard and uncomfortable reef.

Once more the dead silence envelopes us. It is as if we are underwater in the Sea. The Mud Hills and Badlands seem to absorb all sound except a buzzing in my ears from the climb. The hot sun and the climb make us wish we had started earlier. But then a moderating breeze kicks up as we slip and slide picking our way carefully down the reef and return along the Mud Hills the way we came.

T.M. says, "If you're up for it let's go back and do the short Elephant Tree Discovery Trail we passed before turning up

Split Mountain Road. The Elephant trees are found only in Anza-Borrego, southwest Arizona and Northwest Mexico."

My head ached from the rapid climb in the hot bright sun. "A new tree we've never seen before? Count me in." We'd seen the "Knees," now we were on the trail of the Tree.

Elephant Tree Discovery Trail

Parked at the trailhead, we find the trail-guide box empty and wonder how we will recognize the one remaining Elephant Tree growing on this Trail on the desert alluvial fan. This morning's foray into a geologic wonderland left us in a sparsely vegetated section of desert. Now perambulating along the sandy Elephant Tree Discovery Trail, we encounter a beavertail in bloom sporting a pink blossom one-third the size of the cactus. The creosote blooms in a yellow glory and along the way tiny wildflowers show purple and pink tiny blossoms.

We could tell the peak bloom was off the Ocotillos by the yellowed emerald leaves. I feel as droopy as the Ocotillo as we near the end of the loop Trail. A headache sets in with a vengeance and then we see it—there was no doubt we had never before seen this rare Elephant Tree!

The Elephant Tree

Distinct elephantine short thick tapered trunks give way to sturdy crooked branches covered with a straw-hat-colored papery bark peeled back in flakes. Small dull green leaves form the sparse spreading crown. The leaves are adapted to the harsh arid climate

Rare Elephant Tree

and transpire less water. The existence of these trees in this area of Anza-Borrego was first documented in the late 1940's. Since then more Elephant Trees were found to be growing in the nearby Santa Rosa Mountains. Happy and at the end of the Trail, we made note of another trail starting here up the alluvial fan to view more trees. We returned to the car for the drive home up Highway 78.

"Do we have time to stop in Julian for a slice of apple pie?" I pleaded.

"Stop in Julian? We can't drive through Julian— without stopping for pie!"

Seated under the umbrella of pine trees, eating one of our favorite San Diego treats, I remark of the quick passing of twenty years in which we have explored and discovered so many wonders of southern California together. Today, we walked amongst the Elephants and witnessed their rare desert place—a place that makes our lives richer and abundant for its sparseness. I can only dream of the wonders to be shared over the next twenty years together.

~ Travel Notes ~

The Park recommends checking road conditions with Visitor Center staff before venturing out. Four-wheel drive vehicles are best, however a vehicle with good ground clearance will get you there.

To reach the Elephant Tree Discovery Trail, from Highway 78 in Ocotillo Wells drive south on Split Mountain Road 5.9 miles to the Elephant Tree turnoff west (right at the sign.) It is one mile up the road to the Discovery Trail parking area and trailhead. The trail is an easy 1.50-mile sandy loop.

To reach the location where the Elephant Knees hike starts, proceed 2.3 miles farther south on Split Mountain Road to turnoff west (right) at the sign that says Fish Creek Primitive Campground. After another 4.8 miles through Split Mountain, look for the oyster shell wash information panel and "closed to vehicles" sign. Park and start hiking up the wash just east of the information panel. Follow the wash as it meanders toward the Elephant's Knees, taking a right fork that leads you around and behind the Knees. At the back of the knees bushwhack up to the top of the formation. Moderately difficult 4-mile roundtrip takes approximately 2 hours to hike.

The easy 2-mile roundtrip Wind Caves hike starts 3 miles up Split Mountain Road on the Fish Creek Wash.

To continue on to Julian for pie, proceed west on Highway 78 from Ocotillo Wells approximately 35 miles.

A great guidebook to the Anza-Borrego Desert is *The Anza-Borrego Desert Region: A Guide to the State Park and Adjacent Areas of the Western Colorado Desert with Map*, by Diana and Lowell Lindsay.

The Borrego Valley Inn is at 405 Palm Canyon Drive in Borrego Springs. Web site www.borregovalleyinn.com

The Palms at Indian Head and the Krazy Coyote Saloon & Grille are at 2220 Hoberg Road in Borrego Springs web site: www.thepalmsatindianhead.com

Smoked Turkey Sandwich

4 French rolls
1 pound smoked turkey
Sharp mustard
4 slices Provolone cheese

Spread rolls with mustard. Top with cheese and turkey. Refrigerate.

Serves 4.

Epilogue

It was my good fortune to share these special places with family and friends. After each day journey we returned home relaxed, rejuvenated and reconnected to the natural world. We hope sharing our experiences inspires you to get out on foot in San Diego and enjoy the simple pleasure of a picnic. May these journeys give you the same joy they gave us.

Linda Pyle

For book updates and more southern California beach, desert and mountain trails, please visit Linda's website at www.trailwisdom.com.

Also available from Sunbelt Publications by Linda Pyle:

Peaks, Palms & Picnics: Day Journeys in the Mountains & Deserts of Palm Springs & the Coachella Valley of Southern California, ©1999, 2002

Index of Recipes

Appetizers

Grilled Crimini 80

Kalamata Olive and Tuna Tapenade Bruschette 54

Smoked Salmon Spread on Rye...83

Toby's Tapenade 140

Beverages

Hot Mexican Chocolate 23

California Sangria 67

Irish Coffee...74

Cathedral Coffee...91

Breads

Grilled Garlic Toast...112

Mediterranean Bread 16

Port Wine and Basil Butter on Crusty Bread.....................................8

Volcanoes 125

Desserts

Baked Granny Smith Apples 120

Bonfire Candied Apples...22

Doughboys on a Stick..73

Grand Loop Trail Mix 175

Pine Nut Cookies 180

Shirley's Spice Cake..74

S'mores...22

Sunset Trail Chocolate Chip Cookies 186

Susan's Snickerdoodle Cookies..192

Pacific Peaks & Picnics

Main Dish

Pasta

Salads

Sandwiches

Sides

Soups

References and Suggested Reading

Brown, Weston, Buzzell, *Handbook of California Birds*, 1979, Naturegraph Publishers, Inc.

Bell, Suzanne, (photos) *Wildflowers of Cuyamaca Rancho State Park*, 1992, Cuyamaca Rancho State Park Interpretive Assn.

Bell, Suzanne, (photos) *Shrubs of Cuyamaca Rancho State Park*, 1994, Cuyamaca Rancho State Park Interpretive Assn.

Bergen, Frederick W., Clifford, Harold J. and Spear, Steven G., edited by Diane M. Burns, *Geology of San Diego County Legacy of the Land*, 1997, Sunbelt Publications

Cabrillo National Monument Association, *An Account of the Voyage of Juan Rodriguez Cabrillo*, 1999, Cabrillo National Monument Association

Cahill, Joanie Stadtherr, *Anza-Borrego Desert State Park*, 2002 edition, Anza-Borrego Foundation/San Diego Enhancement Program

Clarke, Charlotte Bringle, *Edible and Useful Plants of California*, 1977, University of California Press

Clarke, Herbert, *An Introduction to Southern California Birds*, 1989, Mountain Press Publishing Co.

California Coastal Commission, *California Coastal Access Guide*, 1981, University of California Press

California Coastal Commission, *California Coastal Resource Guide*, 1987, University of California Press

Crooks, Pamela, *Discover Balboa Park: A complete Guide to American's Greatest Urban Park*, 2000, Ridgway Park Publishing

Douglass, Darren, *Diving and Snorkeling Guide to Southern California*, 1994, Gulf Publishing

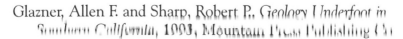

Glazner, Allen F. and Sharp, Robert P., Geology Underfoot in Southern California, 1993, Mountain Press Publishing Co.

Huntington, Glenn, Horticulturist, Desert Garden Series, *The Living Desert*

Jaeger, Edmund C., *Desert Wild Flowers*, 1940, 1941 Stanford University Press

James, George Wharton, *The Wonders of the Colorado Desert*, 1911, Boston Little, Brown, and Company

Jorgensen, Paul, State Park Resource Ecologist, *The Carpenter of Acorns, Visitor Guide Cuyamaca Rancho State Park*, 2001, Cuyamaca Rancho State Park Interpretive Association

Keiser, Mary, *The Sprit of San Pasqual: A Guide to Scenic San Pasqual Valley*, 1986, ———

Kuhn, Gerald G. and Shepard, Francis P. Sea Cliffs, *Beaches, and Coastal Valleys of San Diego County*, 1984, University of California Press

Lee, Melicent Humason, *Indians of the Oaks*, 1937, 1978, 1989, San Diego Museum of Man

LeMenager, Charles R., *Julian City and Cuyamaca Country: A History and Guide to the Past and Present*, 1998, 2001, Eagle Peak Publishing

Lindsay, Lowell and Diana, *The Anza-Borrego Desert Region: A Guide to the State Park and Adjacent Areas of the Western Colorado Desert with Map*, 4th edition, 1998, Wilderness Press

Little, L. Elbert, *National Audubon Society Field Guide to North American Trees, Western Region*, 1980, 1995, Alfred A. Knopf

Robinson, *Ranchos Become Cities*, 1939, San Pasqual Press

Schoenherr, Allan A., *A Natural History of California*, 1992, 1995, University of California Press

Stokes, Donald and Lillian, *Stokes Field Guide to Birds*, 1996, Little, Brown and Company

San Diego Historical Society, www.sandieoghistory.org
———, *Wildflowers of Anza-Borrego Desert State Park*, 1993

Anza-Borrego Desert Natural History Association
———, *San Pasqual Battlefield State Historic Park*, ———, California State Parks

———, *California Native Plant Demonstration Garden*, ———, Balboa Park and Recreation Department

———, *Cuyamaca Rancho State Park Map*, 1988, California Department of Parks and Recreation

———, *Laguna Mountain Recreation Area Trail Map*, 1993, Laguna Mountain Volunteer Association

———, *Trails of the Laguna Mountain Recreation Area*, 2000 revision, Laguna Mountain Volunteer Association

———, *Palomar Mountain State Park*, 1996, California State Parks

———, *Palomar Mountain State Park: Doane Valley Nature Trail*, revised 2000, California State Parks

———, *Mission Trails Regional Park Visitor Center Interpretive Trail*, Self Guided Hike, 2001, Eagle Scout Sean Neugent & City of San Diego Park and Recreation Ranger Staff

———, *Mission Trails Plant Identification Walk*, 2001, City of San Diego Park and Recreation Mission Trails Regional Park Visitor and Interpretive Center

———, *Flowering Plants of Mission Trails Regional Park*, ———, Mission Trails Regional Park Foundation

———, *Mission Trails Regional Park Trail Map*, 2000, Sunbelt Publications, Inc.

———, *Tijuana Estuary Visitor Center: Your Native Plant Garden*, ———, California Parks Department

Sunbelt Publications

"Adventures in the Natural History and Cultural
Heritage of the Californias"

Series Editor–Lowell Lindsay

Southern California Series:

Abracadabra: Mexican Toys (Amaroma) . . . . Aceves
Geology Terms in English and Spanish . . . . Aurand
Geology and Enology of the Temecula Valley (SDAG) . . . . B. Birnbaum, ed.
Water for Southern California (SDAG) . . . . G. Cranham, ed.
Portrait of Paloma: A Novel . . . . Crosby
Orange County: A Photographic Collection . . . . Hemphill
Mexican Slang Plus Graffiti . . . . Jones-Reid
California's El Camino Real and Its Historic Bells . . . . Kurillo
Spanish Lingo for the Savvy Gringo . . . . Reid
Mission Memoirs: Reflections on California's Past . . . . Ruscin
Warbird Watcher's Guide to the Southern California Skies . . . . . . Smith
Campgrounds of Santa Barbara and Ventura Counties . . . . Tyler
Campgrounds of Los Angeles and Orange Counties . . . . Tyler
Jackpot Trail: Indian Gaming in Southern California . . . . Valley

California Desert Series:

Gateway to Alta California . . . . Crosby
Anza-Borrego A To Z: People, Places, and Things . . . . D. Lindsay
The Anza-Borrego Desert Region (Wilderness Press) . L. and D. Lindsay
Geology of the Imperial/Mexicali Valleys (SDAG 1998) . . . L. Lindsay, ed.
Palm Springs Oasis: A Photographic Essay . . . . Lawson
Geology of the EFZ: Hot Springs and
  Tourmalines (SDAG) . . . . Murbach/Hart, eds.
Desert Lore of Southern California . . . . Pepper
Peaks, Palms, and Picnics: Journeys in Coachella Valley . . . . Pyle
Geology of Anza-Borrego: Edge of Creation . . . . Remeika, Lindsay
Paleontology of Anza-Borrego (SDAG 1995) . . . . Remeika, Sturz, eds.
California Desert Miracle: Fight for Parks and Wilderness . . . . . Wheat

Baja California Series:

The Other Side: Journeys in Baja California . . . . Botello
Cave Paintings of Baja California . . . . Crosby
Backroad Baja: The Central Region . . . . Higginbotham

213

Lost Cabos: The Way it Was (Lost Cabos Press) . . . . Jackson
Journey with a Baja Burro . . . . Mackintosh
Houses of Los Cabos (Amaroma) . . . . Martinez, ed.
Houses by the Sea (Amaroma) . . . . Martinez, ed.
Mexicoland: Stories from Todos Santos (Barking Dog Books) . . . Mercer
Roadside Geology of Baja California (Minch & Associates) . . . . Minch
Baja Legends: Historic Characters, Events, Locations . . . . Niemann
Loreto, Baja California: First Capital (Tio Press) . . . . O'Neil
Baja Outpost: The Guestbook from Patchen's Cabin . . . . Patchen
Sea of Cortez Review . . . . Redmond

San Diego Series:
Rise and Fall of San Diego: 150 Million Years . . . . Abbott
Only in America . . . . Alessio
Coastal Geology of San Diego (SDAG) . . . . Stroh, ed.
More Adventures with Kids in San Diego . . . . Botello, Paxton
Weekend Driver San Diego . . . . Brandais
Geology of San Diego County . . . . Clifford, Bergen, Spear
Mission Trails Regional Park Trail Map . . . . Cook
Cycling San Diego . . . . Copp, Schad
La Jolla: A Celebration of Its Past . . . . Daly-Lipe
A Good Camp: Gold Mines of Julian and the Cuyamacas . . . . . . Fetzer
San Diego Mountain Bike Guide . . . . Greenstadt
San Diego Legends . . . . Innis
My Ancestors' Village . . . . Labastida
San Diego Specters: Ghosts, Poltergeists, Tales . . . . Lamb
San Diego Padres, 1969-2001: A Complete History . . . . Papucci
San Diego: An Introduction to the Region . . . . Pryde
San Diego Architecture: From Missions to Modern (SDAF) . . . . . Sutro
Campgrounds of San Diego County . . . . Tyler
Thirst for Independence: The San Diego Water Story . . . . Walker

www.sunbeltbooks.com

Sunbelt Publications

Incorporated in 1988 with roots in publishing since 1973, Sunbelt produces and distributes publications about "Adventures in Natural History and Cultural Heritage." These include natural science and outdoor guidebooks, regional histories and reference books, multi-language pictorials, and stories that celebrate the land and its people.

Our publishing program focuses on the Californias which are today three states in two nations sharing one Pacific shore. Somewhere in the borderland between reality and imagination, a Spanish novelist called adventurers to this region five centuries ago: "Know ye that California lies on the right hand of the Indies, very near to the terrestrial paradise."

Sunbelt books help to discover and conserve the natural and historical heritage of unique regions on the frontiers of adventure and learning. Our books guide readers into distinctive communities and special places, both natural and man-made.

"In the end, we will conserve only what we love,
we will love only what we understand,
we will understand only what we are taught."
— Bouba Dioum, Senegalese conservationist